Integration:
Myth or Reality?

Disability, Handicap and Life Chances Series

Series Editor: Len Barton

DATE DUE

OCT 12 '92			
MAY 19 '94 MAY 1 9 '94			

Disability, Handicap and Life Chances Series

Integration:
Myth or Reality?

Edited by
Len Barton
Bristol Polytechnic

 The Falmer Press

(A member of the Taylor & Francis Group)
London, New York and Philadelphia

UK   The Falmer Press, Falmer House, Barcombe, Lewes,
East Sussex BN8 5DL

USA   The Falmer Press, Taylor & Francis Inc., 242 Cherry Street,
Philadelphia, PA 19106–1906

Selection and editorial material
© copyright L. Barton 1989

First published in 1989

British Library Cataloguing in Publication Data

Integration: myth or reality?
  1. Physically handicapped persons. Social adjustment
  I. Barton, Len
  362.4

ISBN 1–85000–614–8
ISBN 1–85000–615–6 (Pbk.)

Library of Congress Cataloging-in-Publication Data available on request

Typeset in 11/13 Bembo by
The FD Group Ltd, Fleet, Hampshire

Printed in Great Britain by BPCC Wheatons Ltd, Exeter

Contents

To Rachel and Sarai

Preface

The revised papers in this volume were first presented at an International Conference on Disability, Handicap and Policy at Bristol Polytechnic, England in July 1988.

The intention behind the Conference was to provide a forum in which perspectives, research findings, and policy developments could be presented to critical scrutiny. This it was hoped would lead to a strengthening of our commitment to the empowerment of disabled people.

Speakers and delegates came from many different countries.

Grateful thanks are due to Falmer Press, to Christine Cox, Sarah King and Malcolm Clarkson for their important support and encouragement in the planning and running of the Conference.

Thanks are also due to the British Council for offering some financial support for the Conference.

Acknowledgment

I am grateful to Christine Cox for her advice and encouragement that enabled this book to be published.

Len Barton, 1989

Integration: Myth or Reality?

Introduction

Len Barton

The papers in this book focus their attention on the question of integration. One of their underlying themes is that integration is controversial. It is a topic associated with deep felt emotions and heated debates. It raises profound issues far beyond merely educational concerns and is ultimately directing attention to the question of the nature of society.

Within the existing literature dealing with this topic there has been an interest in a narrow range of concerns. Attention has focused on questions of *how* integration can be achieved. Crucial aspects of consideration have been those of resources and access. Little comparative material has been available.

Whilst not denying the importance of resources (Fulcher, Abang), the overall emphasis of the analysis offered in this collection of papers is that of the centrality of ideology and the politics of struggle. This involves the authors in a critique of the unacceptable features of existing systems, relationships and practices. The motivation behind such work is the desire for a society in which social justice is realised and people, disabled people in particular, have real decision-making powers and control over their lives.

In the opening paper Fulcher discusses the question of policy in relation to four countries. Integration, she maintains, needs to be viewed as a struggle over competing objectives between groups involved in unequal power relations. Analysis is focused on those forms of discourse through which perspectives on integration are articulated and legitimated. Particular forms of professionalism are challenged, in that they are identified with practices of control and oppression. In three of the societies discussed, Fulcher argues that the discourse of integration is one of exclusion in that the concerns are with discipline and control. The author is interested in how

1

policy is created, the key factors involved, and the institutional context within which struggles take place.

The question of integration is complex and needs to be examined within a framework in which careful analysis is undertaken of the system of education, including the work context of teachers (Sleeter, Foster, Galloway). In a discussion of her research findings in Wisconsin, USA, Sleeter maintains that teachers face fundamental contradictions in their work. Teachers are actively involved in the sorting functions of schooling, in differentiating pupils from pupils on the basis of ability and this takes place through a process in which it is alleged people are treated fairly. In examining the ways in which teachers deal with the issues that an integrationist policy entails, Sleeter distinguishes between normative and non-normative categories of disability. This raises the question of the extent to which some pupils are discriminated against more than others, as well as how they cope with differential treatment. Sleeter is interested in the degree to which practices within school handicap pupils and how schools deal with those pupils who do not meet the required standards.

It is essential when reference is made to disabled people, that we do not assume a homogeneous perspective. Important differences exist as can be seen from Foster's analysis of deaf people. The author highlights the different forms integration takes for deaf people in the United States. In her own research, which she reports on in this chapter, Foster is interested in the views of deaf pupils on integration and the sorts of experiences they have encountered in different school settings. By investigating the interactions between deaf and hearing pupils, the author argues that deaf pupils were involved in 'trading-options' — i.e. the giving up of one benefit in order to obtain another. Thus, for example, some pupils acknowledged the loss of family life in exchange for personal growth, particularly when it came to making decisions about residential over mainstreamed programmes. In advocating integration it is important to recognise the costs involved, which will entail more pain and difficulties for some people, as opposed to others. This should result, as Foster advocates in this instance, in deaf people being fully involved as partners in the development of the programmes and services they use.

In all cases of policy implementation the question of human agency is crucial. The above papers point to the importance of the teacher's role in this process. Galloway in his contribution maintains that a desire for integration which is fundamentally depicted in terms of children's needs detracts attention from the crucial, but largely unexamined issue, of the teacher's needs. These have to be recognised and met in any effective programme of integration. He combines his discussion of this issue with a consideration of some of the major developments currently taking place in the educational system generally. In doing this he recognises that any identification of needs, including the teacher's, will involve political factors and value judgements. By contextualising his examination within a systems framework, he contends that the extent to which an integrationist policy can be developed and realised will ultimately be contingent upon these wider educational changes and their outcomes.

Whilst recognising this principle, the papers by Vislie, Abang and Goodall also remind the reader that it is not just with school that an integrationist policy must be concerned, but also post-school and the whole of adult life.

The case of Norway presents an interesting study and as the paper by Vislie demonstrates, the question of post-school provision has become an increasingly significant cause for concern. She maintains that in Norway the principle of 'education for all' underpins policy and includes a commitment to positive discrimination. This is necessary in view of the stubborn existence of inequalities within society. In relation to educational provision some of the inequalities are mirrored in the significant difference which exist in policy and practice across counties and even within schools in a specific county. By examining the choices that young people make following post-compulsory schooling and the ways in which options are organised, Vislie highlights some of the difficulties involved in the decision process, the restrictions which operate and how in this complex situation choice turns into allocation and selection. For disabled young people the transition process offers fewer opportunities for choice and more experiences of allocation.

In her discussion of Nigeria and particularly of higher education, Abang draws attention to the question of policy generation in relation to the cultural and economic development of a particular society. Difficulties of implementation are highlighted in terms of the relationships between National and State levels of activity. The analysis also points to the importance of a policy of integration addressing questions of poverty, tribalism and the role of legislation. Not only does this involve the significance of resources and political will on the part of government, but it also places the issue of disability within the context of equal opportunities and makes the question of human rights a matter of priority.

Goodall, in her account of a research project which she undertook in Scotland on the issue of residential homes, maintains that the question of choice and control over one's life are crucial dimensions of any adequate integrationist policy. Where, how, and when people live in particular settings are fundamental issues for disabled people. By considering the experiences and views of a group of disabled adults, Goodall recognises the ways in which professionals have, intentionally and unintentionally, been influential in socialising individuals into various degrees of dependency. This has implications for any move towards independent living, in that some individuals may desire to live in a residential home. This, the author argues, may be an interim measure that will be helpful for some adults on their road to independence.

The paper by Branson and Miller examines the extent to which a particular form of economic and social relations (capitalism), has contributed to the creation of disability. They maintain that within such a process specific value has been placed on being able-bodied in relation to an individual's capacity for work. The role of Science and Medicine in terms of their mechanistic nature and outcomes, receives particular critical evaluation. The lines of thinking entailed and forms of practices involved, the authors argue, have significantly shaped the boundaries of normality and dependency. An integrationist policy must therefore be geared towards its own destruction. The writers have a vision of the world in which the disabled are 'normal', accepted and valued. In such a world integration will not be required for there will be no segregation. The critique they offer demands a transformation of existing social relations, modes of conceptualisations and forms of institutional structures.

The final contribution to the volume by Patricia Potts is different from the rest in that it is a report of a recent visit to China. It contributes to our much needed information on some aspects of policy and practice in this important country. The comparisons which the author draws with those in Britain, and the examples of innovations, tensions and contradictions, provide stimulus for reflection on our assumptions and practices.

If the struggle for integration includes the commitment to create a society in which the necessity for segregation is removed, then the task is complex and demanding. The chapters in this volume do not share a unified perspective, and in that sense they are a reflection of the range of viewpoints available on this issue. However, they do share some significant concerns including the development of a critical analysis of:

  the complex and contradictory nature of policy;

  the gulf which exists between the rhetoric of policy documents, legislation and the realities of practice and degrees of implementation;

  the power struggles between groups/individuals with conflicting vested interests and views of the world;

  the question of rights in relation to disabled people;

  the nature of normality and its impact on our views of difference and disability.

The question of integration involves a series of significant and difficult issues. In their contributions to this volume the writers have highlighted some of these. We must not underestimate the task ahead. People's rights, dignity and opportunity are at stake. What the papers in this book confirm is that there are no slick, easy answers, nor should we be looking for shortcuts to the demanding work still required to be undertaken by all interested parties.

  Hopefully, these chapters will make some small contribution to keeping the debates alive and providing valuable knowledge to inform the struggles of those who, through the commitment to integration, are seeking the realisation of a more humane and equitable form of social life for all.

Chapter 1

Integrate and Mainstream?
Comparative issues in the politics of these policies

Gillian Fulcher

I'm going to survey four government policies on integration and mainstreaming and I shall argue that three of those have got it wrong, quite seriously wrong, and that only one has begun to get it right.

The policies are from the US, the UK, Denmark and Victoria, Australia. They are, in the US, the 1975 US Public Law 94-142, *The Education for All Handicapped Children Act;* in Britain, the 1978 Warnock Report; and its legislation, the 1981 *Education Act;* in Denmark, the Ministry of Education's policy statements about integration and some associated legislation (see the following section); and in Victoria, the report of a Ministerial Review, *Integration in Victorian Education* (1984), which is regarded as the Victorian Labour government's policy on educational services for children with disabilities.

There are, at least superficially, some very clear political/ theoretical differences between these policies: the strategies they recommend, and their intent, or more specifically, their dominant objectives, differ. Moreover, the constitutional and political contexts into which these policies are inserted also vary considerably. Some of these policies consist of legislation, some are reports from Committees or Reviews. Despite these apparent differences between these policies and their contexts, three of these policies have had remarkably similar effects on education practices in their respective education apparatuses. Their major effects are largely not positive as far as integrating or mainstreaming children tagged disabled. How can we explain allegedly different policies having such similar effects? How should we explain the success of the fourth? These questions raise further questions about the nature and politics of government policy. And I think that answering questions about the nature and politics of government level policy is critical in redirecting efforts of educators to integrate or mainstream children called disabled. So, I'll first of all describe the four government policies and outline their differences; second, I'll spell out their major effects in their education apparatuses; third, I'll suggest how we can understand or theorize these effects and fourth, I'll make some suggestions about relevant educational policies for an objective of integration in the sense Tony Booth defines it, that is, the objective to increase the participation of all children in the social and educational life of their peers in regular schools (1981). There are as many meanings of integration or mainstreaming as their proponents have objectives: this places the analysis of integration or mainstreaming policies in a political framework. In this context, integration policy is primarily a struggle between proponents of various objectives. In this chapter, where I refer to integration it is with the objective defined above.

Four government policies

The differences between the four policies lie in their dominant objectives, their political discourses and in the strategies they recommend.

For the US, it's very clear that the advocates of PL 94-142 intended achieving a better deal both for children in special education and for those excluded from regular and special education. Their dominant objective was one of radical change and they drew on the wider discourse about the rights of minority groups in the US and inserted this theme in their tactics for changing special education. The advocates of this better deal chose a legal strategy in their struggle to achieve their objectives. A series of key legislative decisions in various States about inequities in special education preceded the passing of PL 94-142. The law included statements about the 'special educational needs' of eight million handicapped children: its aim was to ensure 'free appropriate education' for all handicapped children and 'due procedures' or procedural safeguards to be followed at various levels in the education apparatus were to be the means to achieve this. Thus the Act legislated for extensive reporting procedures at other levels, in State Education Agencies and Local School Districts (Gerry, 1985). A key mechanism the law proposed was that a team, including parents, should draw up an

Individualized Education Plan, an IEP: note the professional language both in Individualized Education Plan and in the notion of 'appropriate'.

Public Law 94-142 drew on contrary discourses: a democratic discourse about rights (thus team decisions) and a professional discourse whose language and practice (as conveyed in 'appropriate') implies someone has the expertise to judge what is appropriate. This latter discourse can be called professionalism as opposed to a rights or democratic discourse. These are antithetical discourses. Their presence in one policy indicates not contradictions but contending objectives, competing discourses, of those formulating the policy. Discourse is a tactic deployed to achieve some objective: it is essentially political, never merely technical though the use of professionalism's technobabble such as 'IEP', 'special educational needs', and 'appropriate', obscure the politics embedded in this vocabulary: as Sally Tomlinson (1987) and Peter Beilharz (1987) have recently said, we need to look critically at the language that is used.

In contrast to PL 94-142, the Warnock Report and the 1981 *Education Act* are much more politically equivocal about an objective to promote integration. They are conservative policy: as Warnock has said: 'we fudged integration but we fudged it as a matter of policy' (1978). As a number of people have noted, it advocated more of the same; in fact its major implications were to extend special education (Tomlinson, 1985). Kirp has noted the professionalism deployed in this policy (1983)[1]. What is not so often noted is the entrenched medically-based discourse on disability which informs both the Warnock Report and the legislation. The notion of special educational needs merely camouflages this and is a professional newspeak, fresh technobabble, for disability: the 1981 Act defined special educational needs ultimately in terms of disability. What we have in the Warnock Report is a medically-based, individualistic deficit model or discourse being extended to 20 per cent of the school population. Such language constructs or articulates the problem in a certain way. It's clear that this construction — official statements saying that it's all right or even desirable to see 20 per cent of schoolchildren as having special educational needs — is an extraordinarily political act. And what the language, this articulation, distracts us from considering is alternative perspectives on the issues: for instance, it distracts us from noticing that key people in the education apparatus, the teachers of teachers, have failed to provide trainee teachers with the competence to teach more than 80 per cent of the school population. The politics of marginalizing 20 per cent of the school population cannot be allocated only to the teachers of teachers however. There are other institutionalized bases for this marginalization and exclusion which I'll take up later. Overall, the Warnock Report's equivocal intent, its professionalism and its discourse on disability as applicable to 20 per cent of the school population, far outweigh its much weaker discourse on parents' rights as partners. The main strategy which the Warnock Report and the 1981 Act advocate to achieve their equivocal objective is extensive reporting procedures in Local Education Authorities. In this respect, it shares broadly similar strategies to PL 94-142's reporting or monitoring procedures.

In contrast to the British policy, *Integration in Victorian Education* is politically far from equivocal, and though it too draws on some opposing discourses or frameworks, it has a predominantly democratic discourse (its guiding principle is every child has a right to regular education) and a clear critique of the historically established professional control of special education practices. The Report's dominant objective was democratic: to restore parity of treatment in the educational apparatus for those children tagged disabled. This democratism underpinned the critique of professionalism: thus the report rejected the concepts of professionalism (assessment, placement, 'in the child's best interest', etc.) but the struggles in Review meetings over this issue are revealed, for example, in the Extension Notes: these were inserted ten minutes before the report was presented to the Minister. They represent the struggle between the teacher union representative's objective (to contain the focus on children) and the parent representative's objective (to have equal numbers of parents and professionals in the proposed participatory decision-making structures.

Within the Victorian education apparatus, the Victorian policy was widely received as controversial, even as outrageous by some (its main writer should have been hung, drawn and quartered was one comment of a senior bureaucrat not on the Review). Special educators and bureaucrats in other Australian States saw the policy as an extreme document whereas the Commonwealth Schools Commission (a former Federal educational agency now disbanded in the restructuring of education) stated it was a significant document which represented 'the first Australian attempt to reconstruct the educational process, one which was based in a clear social theory of the adverse effects on children who are segregated' (1985, 25). Those responses to that policy document indicate some of the politics of policy making which *follow* government policy[2]. That banal point is nevertheless missed, or perhaps avoided, by those on all positions of the political spectrum when they later seek to explain the 'failure' of government policy.

What also distinguishes the Victorian policy from say, the British policy, is the report's recommendations that participatory decision making structures be set up at all levels in the Victorian educational apparatus. Thus it was recommended that Enrolment Support Groups be set up at school level, Integration Committees at Regional level and so on. Enrolment Support Groups and Committees on integration at other levels in the education apparatus were thus to be the means for achieving the rights of children formerly marginalized in, or excluded from, education: such proposals drew on fairly traditional democratic socialist strategy. These were very different proposals from those in the Warnock Report on how professionals should help parents as partners.

In the Victorian Review, the proponents of democratism did not have an easy time. The struggle in Review meetings, for example, over membership issues of these participatory decision-making structures (were professionals to dominate membership or were the members to consist of parents, advocate and two professionals only?) indicates the politics of policy-production at government level, despite the Minister later presenting the policy as a consensus report. Looking back now, the Victorian proposals for participatory decision making structures seem naive politics but they were in line with the Victorian Labour government's general policy and they were, at the time, hotly debated, and much time, energy and group dynamic ploys were expended in attempting to influence these decisions. What was happening of course was that Review members, as representatives of wider groups in the education apparatus, were seeking to achieve the objectives of these groups, whether these were the relatively powerless parent groups or the very powerful (in Victoria) teacher unions and senior bureaucrats. It would be naive to argue that the representatives' objectives were consistently to give marginalized, excluded children a better education.

Despite these struggles surfacing in the report's recommendations, the Victorian report was seen as radical in its strategies, aims and critique of professionalism. I've described a little of the politics of the policy production at government level because it indicates not only the kinds of struggles played out in the government arena but also the struggles which are replayed in other arenas in the education apparatus following the government issuing what we call its policy.

The Danish policy on integration differs in various ways from the other three policies. It consists, firstly, of various statements issued by the Danish Ministry of Education, its officers and consultants (Hansen, J., 1982, 1984; Hansen, O., 1981, no date: A, no date: B; Ministry of Education, 1986; Pedersen no date: A, no date: B, post-1982). The objective in these is clearly to promote integration through emphasizing the centrality of pedagogic issues. The Danish Ministry has no legislation for integration nor does it recommend extensive procedures at other levels, whether these are of the reporting kind (as in the UK), monitoring and team decisions (as in the US), or participatory decision structures (as in Victoria). The language in the Ministry's statements — how it articulates what has to be done to achieve integration — is significantly different from the discourses in the US, UK and Victorian policies. It dismisses the terms of the discourse of handicap/disability: it states that children cannot be divided into those with handicaps and those without; that a connection between 'diagnosis' and placement cannot be sustained (Hansen, J., 1982, 156-7; Hansen, O., B:4); and that 'categorization is false and artificial and very often not only meaningless but a real dangerous trap in which children for years or maybe their lives can be tangled by a totally wrong or misleading assessment' (Hansen, J., 1984, 10). But this dismissal of a discourse on handicap is not an insidious linguistic device for encapsulating a larger proportion of Danish schoolchildren as deficient in some way, through, for instance, having 'special educational needs'. Rather, it presents the issue as **educational: all children are firstly pupils.** This immediately raises matters of how and what to teach in regular classrooms. So the Danish discourse raises issues of **pedagogy** not disability/handicap; of **competence** not professionalism.

A second significant difference between the Danish policy and the US and UK legislative strategies, is that the Danish Ministry's view was that legislating for integration was quite counter-productive. Instead, the Danish Ministry consulted very widely with those involved for a number of years before it sought to introduce its policy.

A third difference is that the Danish Ministry funds and researches pedagogic issues in successful integration programs and then provides that information to schools. This focus on curriculum, and on teaching and researching good practices, distinguishes the Danish Ministry's approach from that of say, the Victorian Ministry where the nature of research is peculiar. What often happens in Victorian government educational research is that very small amounts of money are made available to one thoroughly overworked researcher who undertakes a 'research project' which includes a great deal of political work and 'consulting' with various constituencies, and what results is a small publication which describes one or two marvellous achievements in a very few schools but does not theorize that achievement, so there is little useful knowledge conveyed to readers of the booklet.

Fourth, the Danish Ministry's statements do not deploy professionalism. By that, I mean that the language, the discourse which imputes expertise to professionals and which relegates decisions about 'appropriateness' to experts is not used. The Danish Ministry's position here is consistent with its focus on children firstly as pupils. That statement belongs not to professionalism but concerns central educational matters: how do we teach all pupils? That is a matter of **technical competence** not professionalism. This focus does not eliminate the possibility that professionalism may be deployed in other arenas in the Danish educational apparatus. What is significant is the Ministry's concern with technical competence.

In sum, there are important differences between these four government policies. The US, Victorian and Danish policies seek to promote integration but they deploy different policies/discourses and either recommend or adopt different strategies in an attempt to ensure that integration happens in schools. The US policy's recommended strategies and procedural safeguards and discourses are those of democratism *and* professionalism; the Victorian report contains a predominantly democratic discourse, but professionalism surfaces every now and again in, for instance, prevalence rates of alleged disabilities, though the key strategy recommended was a democratic socialist one of participatory decision-making structures or groups. The Warnock Report and the 1981 *Education Act* are politically conservative in their objectives, contain heavily entrenched professionalism and a medically based discourse on disability which is extended to 20 per cent of the school population; its main recommended implementation strategy is statementing procedures.

Beyond these differences, the institutional contexts into which these policies are inserted vary. The US, the UK and the Victorian policies each talk of rights of parents and/or children (though they clearly differ in how seriously they engage with this issue) but the UK and Victorian policies, in contrast to the US, have no legal or constitutional basis for enacting such rights: in such a context 'rights' are fictional. The Danish policy does not talk about rights but its wider political context is characterized by historically lengthy and vigorous social democratic politics (Castles and McKinlay, 1979).

Thus strong social democratic politics have been present in political struggles in Denmark. This compares with the relative absence of social democratic politics in the US (despite its Constitution and its self-conscious democratism), in the UK and in Victoria[3]. Thus while the history of integration can be read in all four countries as an historical struggle between the proponents of integration and the proponents of segregation, the social democratic political discourse in Denmark provides a quite different wider context for integration struggles in education. I think it's fair to say that while equality, as a general objective, is an ephemeral aim (see, for example, Hindess, 1987), an objective of equality has informed political and educational debate in Denmark far more extensively than it has in Britain, the US or Victoria. The wider political culture in Denmark is more favourable to struggles in the educational apparatus for equality and integration than is the case in the other three countries, although the constitutional basis of rights in North America would appear, at least superficially, to provide a potentially favourable institutional context for the enactment of the educational rights of these children.

What are the major effects of these government policies?

Despite apparently important differences between the US, the UK and the Victorian policies, their major effects in their respective education apparatuses are extraordinarily similar.

First, they have **amplified** enormously the range of **bureaucratic procedures** surrounding integration or mainstreaming issues. The evidence for this is overwhelming. In the US, in State Education Agencies, in Local Education Districts and in schools (Mehan, 1984; Mehan *et al.,* 1981), there has been extensive bureaucratization of practices surrounding mainstreaming: committees meet, forms are completed, gestures are made at team decisions, etc. All this has very little to do with better teaching practices for children labelled handicapped. What it has to do with is formal, political responses to procedural requirements which the law or a report imposes: these responses merely *comply* with the law as opposed to achieving the *aims* of the law (Hargrove *et al.,* 1983; Berman, 1986; Kirp and Jensen, 1986). This is an important point which I'll return to later.

In the UK too there has also been an increase in bureaucratic procedures via, for example, the 1981 Act's requirements about Statementing, and there are numerous reports about an increase in time-consuming procedures surrounding integration issues in LEAs.

In Victoria, integration issues and practices have been extensively bureaucratized following the 1984 report, despite wider education policy statements from the Victorian Labour government that they will reduce bureaucracy (Ministerial Paper No. 1). It would be possible, for instance, to spend all one's workdays attending the numerous committee meetings on integration in various arenas (in schools, in Regional Offices, in teacher union meetings, etc.). In one Regional Office, for instance, a committee met for a full fortnight to consider 383 applications for teachers' aides: imagine too, the resources spent on these bureaucratic procedures in receiving and photostatting these applications and in paying the salaries for, say, ten committee members for a fortnight. This point is relevant to arguments about resources being short for integration.

Two particularly good examples of bureaucratizing integration issues in Victoria occur in the regulation of Enrolment Support Group procedures and in the practice of 'delayed admission'. Where Enrolment Support Groups are concerned, an early memorandum from the Ministry (No. 34 of 13 March 1986) on guidelines for these groups was nine pages long and included a diagram of seven sets of sequences, two of which had three subsets; a more recent memorandum (17 August 1987) revising these procedures is nineteen pages long and more directive than that of 13 March 1986. (These memoranda of course are an attempt by central bureaucrats to intervene in the politics surrounding Enrolment Support Groups in schools). 'Delayed admission' is a *newly introduced status* for a child tagged disabled who has been deemed in Enrolment Support Group meetings to need a teacher's aide or some other resource which is not available. The child is allowed to enrol but not to enter the school until resources are in place (memorandum from the Minister of Education, 20 May 1985). Many principals, outside the arena in which they demand extra resources, will admit that such demands are political. This bureaucratically brilliant practice of delayed admission illustrates very clearly the *increased regulation* of children tagged disabled following an *integration* policy. These bureaucratic practices are of course intensely political.

Thus bureaucratization is inseparable from a *second* effect: the US, UK and Victorian policies have **politicized** practices surrounding mainstreaming or integration. In the US this is demonstrated by the extensive litigation which has followed PL 94-142. In Britain, the application of the notion of special educational needs to 20 per cent of schoolchildren, for the majority of whom no known impairment exists, is an extremely political act; and studies such as that of

Goacher *et al.* (1986), which note what they call the 'remaking' of policy in educational arenas outside the Warnock Committee and Parliament, attest to this increased politicization. In Victoria, the introduction of 'delayed admission' is bureaucratically brilliant and politically significant: this practice makes increasingly tentative the lives of children tagged disabled whose lives are already more than usually contingent on those who hold power in bureaucratic contexts. The decision to introduce delayed admission was made by senior bureaucrats and teacher unions, and a related decision to continue allocating significant funds to the segregated section was made, of course, in light of the politics of teacher union discourse about appropriate teacher ratios and working conditions, politics in which discourses about professionalism, disability and unionism are deployed.

The tactics Victorian bureaucrats deploy is also illustrated in the way they present integration issues to parents. This is to talk about shortages and about 'extra' allocations made in a time of economic restraint. The Victorian Minister of Education and the bureaucracy have been hugely successful in persuading parents that lack of resources for their child is the key issue. It is not. Moreover, resources are not as short as is made out: resources are absorbed in bureaucratic procedures (the Committee mentioned earlier which met for a fortnight, for instance) and funds, at four to five times per head those allocated for a child in a regular school, continue to be allocated to the segregated sector (Fulcher, 1988). These decisions, as Booth (1982) implies for Norway, are decisions made *in* educational apparatuses: they indicate the making of policy at all levels.

Third, these three policies have **escalated the proportion of schoolchildren tagged disabled.** This is less true in the US, where the law states that only 12 per cent can be officially identified as handicapped (though of course the legislation cannot control the amount of informal labelling), than it is of the UK, for instance, where central level statements suggest 20 per cent should be thus categorized. In Victoria, the Warnock statistic is widely deployed in debate, while in schools, children in regular classrooms have suddenly been termed 'integration children'. Thus their presence, their actual right to being there, has been challenged (Tschiderer, 1986) since their new identity presumes extra resources are, at least potentially, required. About 3,000 students in regular schools in Victoria are now labelled as 'integration children', a category of disability that did not exist before the 1984 report (Lewis, 1988).

'Integration child' is one of the local Victorian variants for 'special educational needs'. Labelling a child 'integration child' has been used to suspend children from school until the resources (an extra teacher, or teacher's aide) deemed as necessary for that child have been provided. The Ministry of Education's memorandum of 29 April 1986 attempts to intervene in these school politics or policies. As already suggested, these memoranda are attempts by central level bureaucrats to intervene in the political processes at school level. Central to these school politics is a resource struggle between teacher unions and their employer, the Ministry, with demands which, out of the arena in which they make the demand, principals will often acknowledge is entirely political. So one consequence of integration policies in the UK and Victoria has been to extend a discourse of disability to more children even via such allegedly benevolent labels as 'integration child'. All of this language — 'integration child', 'special educational needs' — is of course political and an instance of language as 'both the instrument and object of power' (Codd, 1988, 241).

The **increased resource struggle** which has followed both the UK and Victorian policies constitutes a fourth development following these central level policies. In the politics of resource struggles, professionalism is deployed, with its theme of 'expert with clearly defined responsibilities': this leads to the notion of 'my child not yours' (or vice versa) and is connected with discourses on disability and on unionism with its themes of teacher student ratios. Professionalism fragments its clients: in medical professionalism it divides people into parts of a body and in educational professionalism it divides the school population into 'types' of children to be taught by different types of teachers. Professionalism constructs its clients: in medicine as patients, not people with a body, and in education as children with alleged disabilities rather than as pupils.

A fifth effect of the US and the Victorian policies is their clear failure to achieve a better educational deal for children formerly excluded, or at risk of being excluded, from regular education. This is so despite the fact that in both education apparatuses some children are now in regular schools who might not have been there before these policies. Their presence may only indicate locational integration: moreover, their being in regular schools cannot be attributed *directly* to these policies beyond the fact that for some of these children their parents may have been encouraged, by the apparent support and tactics these policies offered, to pursue their objectives. But this sort of event — parents pursuing their objectives and some of them getting their child into a regular school — is how the system and its politics worked *before* these policies were made.

The evidence that a better deal has not been achieved is available for the US, the UK and the Victorian policies. In the US, Gerry, a Washington lawyer prominent in struggles for a better deal, notes, as do many others, the failure of PL 94-142 to achieve its aims. He proposes more regulation of education practices surrounding mainstreaming and even suggests *behavioural measures of agency responses* should be used to monitor the implementation activities of State Education Agency bureaucrats (Gerry, 1985). This, however, is to miss the point which is that *law* can only *regulate* practices surrounding educational aims but it cannot directly control pedagogic practice. American educators, writing about PL 94-142 from an educational rather than a legal stance, repeatedly present research findings suggesting that what matters in getting a better deal for all children is teaching practices and the policies in *schools*.

Evidence for the failure of integration in Britain can be drawn from the work of Swann (1985) and Booth (1981) who have provided statistics about the categories of children who have been increasingly segregated from regular schools following the Warnock Report and the 1981 Act. In Victoria, there is general agreement that an integration objective, despite all the activity surrounding the issues, has not occurred. What has emerged in the Victorian apparatus is an intensified debate, and increasingly bureaucratized and politicized practices. There is no clear evidence that children from segregated settings have moved to regular schools but there is evidence that the number of children marginalized has increased (Tschiderer, 1986; Lewis, 1988).

None of this is to argue against the fact that some children with, or perceived as having, impairments are getting a very good deal in regular schools. But this has always been the case. For instance, Booth, in 1983, noted that examples of integrating children with the range of impairments could be found somewhere in a school in Britain; and argued that: 'The overwhelming conclusion is that where integration does not happen it is because people with the power to make the changes do not want children with disabilities in our schools' (1983, 266). Such practices indicate that successful integration practices in schools are independent of government level policy. In Victoria, the closure of a new rural Special Developmental School (a segregated school for children with more severe impairments) was achieved between 1979 and 1981 by its principal, initially against the wishes of the local community who had helped build the school, and well before the 1984 Ministerial Report, *Integration in*

Victorian Education.

Sixth, it is also clear that these three **government level policies do not control what happens in schools:** see, for example, Booth's comments for the UK; the Victorian evidence is also clear on this as is the American research (Fulcher, forthcoming). It is in schools that critical decisions are made which initiate integration or exclusions. Teachers' decisions about integration depend on their competence and commitment, on their objectives and on their colleagueship with other teachers (Hargrove *et al,* 1983). Schools, allegedly regulated by these government policies, respond differently to these policies. Such responses show that schools have some important independence from government level integration or mainstreaming policies.

Finally, the Danish Ministry's policy appears to have had none of the first five effects which have followed the other three policies. The evidence shows that the Danish Ministry's policy has had a different outcome: it appears not to have increased bureaucratic regulation nor to have politicized or professionalized issues surrounding integration struggles. This is not to say that the Danish Ministry has thereby dissolved integration struggles in schools or local arenas, merely that it has focused attention on the central issues and provided some information on how to solve them.

In sum, successful integration appears to have very little to do with issuing central government policies. Whether these policies are highly regulatory or prescriptive, as in the US and UK, or more clearly democratic as in Victoria, and whether they consist of legislation or reports or both, each of these three policies has systematically produced bureaucratic regulation and politicization and at least two of them have led to more marginalization of an increasing proportion of the school population. How can we explain such similar effects from apparently substantially different government policies? The answer lies in the politics of educational apparatuses and understanding these politics requires some theorizing about the nature of policy, including government policy, as a form of intervention in social life.

Explaining these effects

Here I shall argue that we have to look very critically, and with relatively new theoretical lenses, at our assumptions about the nature of government policy and at the arguments — the debate — about disability. Notions such as a gap between rhetoric and practice, or that policy is like the layers of an onion[4] hardly illuminate our understanding of the processes involved and provide little direction for moving from the failure of these government level policies.

First, government level policies are only one level of policy making in the educational apparatus: we should not expect government level education policies, for instance on integration, to control what happens at other levels such as schools. Policies are made at all levels, for instance, in teacher union arenas, in school committees and in encounters between teacher and child or teacher and parent. Power, in other words, is diffused throughout the educational apparatus and is manifest in the decisions which social actors make and on which they largely base their actions. This view draws on the work of Hindess (1986, 1987), Demaine (1981), and Culley and Demaine (1983), and the theoretical categories of social actor are clearly spelt out in Hindess (1986).

Second, government policy such as the reports and legislation I've discussed, are only *one* type of intervention or practice, albeit an important one, in the educational apparatus. It is useful to put all social practices in a political analysis. Social life may be theorized as a series of practical projects, in each of which we struggle to achieve our objectives. Such an analysis makes no value judgement about the ends we seek to attain. Importantly, the means we deploy to achieve our objectives are based in a social theory of how the world works — however mistaken our social theory might be — and this will include a discourse we deploy to achieve our objectives. Failing to achieve our objectives may be due to our misunderstanding the nature of our project, that is, to an inadequate social theory of how the aspect of social life we hope to influence works: we may present the project via the wrong discourse or we may misunderstand the nature of politics in state apparatuses, for instance, by assuming that it is the law, in some over-riding sense, rather than politics and the use of power, as the evidence from researching these policies suggests, that governs our lives.

Thus all social practices, even the most mundane, have certain attributes as *social practices* which define their character and constitute their limits and thus the extent to which they work as 'successful' intervention in social life. The notion of intervention is often confined to political action by government but in a real sense all social practices are interventions: we seek by our decisions and actions and discourses to achieve an objective. Once we dissolve the distinction between government or national level policy and other allegedly more mundane actions of citizens and see each as social practices whose outcomes depend on objectives and on an adequate understanding of how something, for instance an education apparatus, works, then I think we can make sense of the counter effects and contrary practices which have followed the US, UK and Victorian government policies on integration or mainstreaming.

Each of these policies misunderstands the social world, though perhaps the British case less so. The US advocates of a better deal assumed law can achieve *substantive* educational change, that is, better teaching practices, whereas the evidence shows it can only regulate procedures. The Victorian Report is based in a mistaken social theory that participatory decision-making can achieve democratic outcomes: this premise ignores the power relations between groups in the educational apparatus and the undemocratic objectives for which power can be deployed at any level in an educational apparatus. The Victorian Review also appears to have misunderstood the politics of consulting with those who would be affected by an integration policy. It consulted expediently during the relatively short life of the Review. This compares with the Danish practice of consulting over a long period prior to introducing integration as a central level policy. The apparent success of the Danish use of the political process suggests that some of the political responses and moral panics which followed the Victorian Report could have been averted with more adequate discussion of what was really involved.

So one reason for the failure of the US, UK and Victorian policies is that they were based in a mistaken social theory. This social theory should have included the notion that policy is made at all levels and that, given this, it is important to write a government level policy of the kind which reduces the subsequent conflict in the education apparatus — conflict which Offe sees as one of the functions of state policy — and which thereby promotes an objective of integration in the sense outlined. Clearly the Danish Ministry did a better job of working out the politics of all this.

The second factor which contributed to the failure of these three government policies relates to their discourses on disability, whether this found expression in the notion of handicap (as in the US), special educational needs (Britain) or in the notions of impairment, disability or problems in schooling, as in Victoria[5]. This derives from the view that the language deployed in a national policy, for instance, is a key factor in its outcomes.

Discursive practices surrounding disability are inevitably about exclusion (Shapiro, 1981). Disability denotes deficit, loss, difference, marginality: it contains a political logic of exclusion which, given the institutionalized bases in the educational apparatuses for excluding some children from regular schools, can be deployed whenever someone in power makes a decision which lends itself to the exclusion of that child. As suggested earlier, discourses articulate the world in certain ways. As Shapiro puts it, 'Taken as a whole, the set of discursive practices in which the concept of disability is lodged provides the rules of exclusion that constitute the meaning of disability' (1981,1987).

Moreover, given its connection with exclusion **disability is a political construct of oppression**. This is Abberley's argument (1987). The themes of difference, loss and marginal identity, combined with the political logic of extra resources, exclude the more appropriate themes of pedagogy and teaching practices. A discourse on disability is clearly the wrong choice where the objective is meaningful integration. To move away from exclusion, different themes and different questions must replace this discourse. The relevant themes here are those of teaching styles and the relevant questions should focus on solving the problems which lead to exclusion.

A discourse of disability deflects attention from these issues. **Integration is controversial because it is about discipline, curriculum and pedagogy; it is not about disability**. In raising issues of curriculum and discipline integration thus raises the two great historical concerns of teachers, while pedagogy is no less problematic, as Simon has argued in his chapter 'Why no Pedagogy in England?' (Simon, 1985), an argument which seems applicable to Australia. Thus integration policy raises central issues in education: it is these issues rather than disability which constitute the real politics of integration objectives.

While a discourse on disability is inconsistent with the central issues in integration, it promotes a medical politics of impairment and thus deflects our attention from the fact that disability is a procedural category of oppression. Its procedural, therefore political, status is clear if we suspend presumptions about the presence of impairment when we talk of disability, an analytical move we need to make if we consider the ludicrous nature of the claim inferred that 20 per cent of the school population have an impairment.

Further, a discourse on disability, by deflecting our attention from the curriculum, also means we are less likely to locate a key institutional basis for exclusion. Thus **it is the failure in the educational apparatus by those whose concern it should be, to**

provide an inclusive curriculum, and to provide teachers with a sense of competence in such a curriculum, which constructs the politics of integration and a key basis for exclusion.

The third factor in explaining the politics of these policies in their educational apparatuses is the deployment of professionalism. We need to note however, that *not all professionals use professionalism*. But professionalism, as discourse, is tactic, and one which has been deployed historically by an increasing number of occupational groups to gain control of an area of occupational life: nurses, teachers and social workers are perhaps the most recent examples and trade unionism is another discourse, practice and tactic which may be deployed for or against integration. In education apparatuses such as the Victorian apparatus, in the context of a discourse about disability, professionalism has been deployed with unionism to create a discourse about resources and this constructs the politics of exclusion.

Conclusions

The effects these four policies have had show that government level written policy is important *not* because it controls substantive educational matters, such as *how* to teach, but because of the nature of the debate it sets up and the politics it initiates at other levels in its educational apparatus. Government policies in the US, UK and Victoria have set up a counter-productive debate and politics *if* their objectives were integration in Booth's sense. (It seems that this was the objective in the US and Victorian policies.) The Danish Ministry's policy had a different outcome.

Clearly too, these government policies do not control schools in any direct sense as far as teaching styles and pedagogic practices are concerned, yet these are obviously central to real integration practices. Thus what matters in education practice is *how, what* and *where* to teach. Government level policy controls little of this: it may control some of *what* gets taught via, for instance, establishing a core curriculum, but even there it cannot control how teachers engage with the curriculum, and how they engage with it is also part of what gets taught. The government level integration and mainstreaming policies discussed here do not control *how* teachers teach students tagged disabled. Nor is it clear that government level education policy controls *where* students get taught. In Victoria, the government policy clearly suggested resources should be redeployed from the segregated sector to regular schools. But in other arenas, policies made by senior bureaucrats and teacher union representatives, such as 'delayed admission' and continuing to fund segregated schools at four to five times the amount allocated per child to regular schools, indicates that *where* these students are taught is clearly a policy decision emanating from power struggles in arenas in education apparatuses.

Moreover *what* these students are taught depends in part on *where* but also, importantly, by whom: **social actors in other arenas** — bureaucrats, teacher union representatives, and teachers — **are also key policy makers.** This point gets lost in the focus on, and in the escalated politics which have followed, three of these four government level policies. The importance attributed to government level integration or mainstreaming policies in the US, UK and Victoria thus seems mistaken. A major conclusion from researching the effects of these policies affirms social actors' policies at other levels are possibly more important than government level policy. This includes the point that other research makes: in integration policy, it seems that *teachers matter at least as much as government level policy.*

This analysis suggests a number of ways or means for achieving an objective of integration.

First, teachers need to have a greater sense of, and *technical competence* in, how to teach; and second, they need to be taught that professionalism is essentially a tactic to *control* educational practices, a tactic deployed in classrooms, committees, and a whole range of educational arenas and that consequently professionalism is separate from what may be called technical competence. Third, the focus on disability should be dropped: disability is essentially a political construct which has a variable relationship to impairment. Moreover, disability is enmeshed in relations of exclusion and, as Paul Abberley has argued, it is a category of oppression (1987). We therefore need to replace the theme of disability with a focus on pedagogic issues. These three points suggest that the teachers of teachers should teach a curriculum for all students and that they should abandon their courses on disability where these present some children as different, and as therefore requiring a separate curriculum and a separate pedagogy. Thus **teacher training institutions are a key institutional base for the politics of excluding** or marginalizing increasing numbers of **schoolchildren.** Fourth, dropping the focus on disability and instituting an integrated curriculum through changes in teacher training institutions means re-organizing and undermining key institutional bases of disability and exclusion in educational apparatuses; these include the existence of segregated schools, a separate profession, and separate special education courses. Such a task is far from easy. But if professionalism and a discourse on disability have been the key discourses and tactics deployed to institutionalize exclusion, to set up separate schools, and a separate profession and curricula, then part of the politics of undermining the institutional bases of exclusion lies in decoding professionalism for the tactic it is and in recognizing it whenever and wherever it's deployed.

At the same time, we need to reassess the political effects of a debate about disability and to consider the benefits of replacing it with a discourse about curriculum. This is already occurring in a number of the Open University texts. Disability connotes need, and need has been a powerful concept for organizing welfare state provision, but the evidence increasingly suggests that where allocation is made on the basis of need this results in the exclusion of those tagged needy. This is the case for the various tags which have emerged in integration policies (special education needs, integration child, etc). Need is therefore not about privileged provision as Stone (1984) argues: its real politics are about exclusion. The attempt to challenge these politics via a discourse on rights has failed, for instance, in North America and in Victoria where professionalism has been a powerful tactic in blocking an integration objective. In contrast, the Danish Ministry's focus on pedagogic issues for pupils appears to avoid these politics.

Finally, there are two main arguments against professionalism. Since it excludes the person most affected from taking part in that decision, it is anti-democratic, if by democracy we mean being able to take part fully in decisions that affect us, rather than have them imposed on us. Secondly, professionalism as tactic, where it is deployed as a retreat from responsibility (your child not mine) is ultimately self-defeating, since as Jamrozik notes, citing from a recent book on the welfare state, 'there simply can be no guarantee for the security of the self if it does not take into account the well-being of the other' (1988, 27).

Further, these claims against professionalism imply a critique of bureaucratic practices in educational apparatuses. Bureaucracy, as a form of organization, presents itself as staffed by 'experts', with clearly demarcated areas of responsibility: the notion of expertise increases the likelihood that professionalism will be deployed. Bureaucratic forms of organization are inherently anti-democratic:

Weber feared the iron-cage of bureaucracy posed the greatest threat to the Western value of individual freedom (Gerth and Wright Mills, 1970). In research in Victorian schools democratic policies have foundered on bureaucratic processes (Rizvi *et al.*, 1987). The present research revealed similar processes. Abolishing such practices, moving towards locally made decisions, and providing technical, pedagogic knowledge for teachers and trainee teachers about inclusive teaching practices are clearly ways out of the counter-productive regulation and escalated politics which three of these four government level policies have produced.

Notes

1 Kirp's analysis is less political than the analysis of discourse as tactic which is employed here. He uses the term professionalization to refer to the policy choice to use professionals to implement the policy. In the political struggles model outlined here (see later section) professional-ism is discourse, thus tactic, deployed to achieve some objective; professionalization is the historical struggle occupational groups engage in (and deploy professionalism in) to gain control of an area of occupational life.

2 Beilharz has argued: 'Now is the time for debate, for contestation difference, articulation as well as aggregation — because politics comes *before* policy' (1987, 404). But it is also the case that politics *follow* policy.

3 For a comparison of Australia and some Western European countries, see Castles (1985).

4 On this see Whitmore (1984) cited in Welton and Evans (1986, 213).

5 While the Report sought to distinguish these terms and to make a critique of school/teaching practices via the somewhat clumsy notion of problems in schooling, the struggle to deploy problems in schooling as a new deficit tag for children emerged strongly in the Report (see Extension, Note 2) and in struggles later in the Victorian educational apparatus. For some people, problems in schooling has become synonymous with 'socially and emotionally handicapped'. This merely illustrates the *tactical* nature of discourses.

References

ABBERLEY, P. (1987) 'The Concept of Oppression and the Development of a Social Theory of Disability', *Disability, Handicap and Society*, 2, 1, pp. 5-20.

BEILHARZ, P. (1987) 'Reading politics: Social theory and social policy', *Australia and New Zealand Journal of Sociology*, 23, 3, pp. 388-406.

BERMAN, P. (1986) 'From Compliance to Learning: Implementing Legally

Induced Reform', in KIRP, D.L. and JENSEN, D.N. (Eds) *School Days, Rule Days,* Lewes, Falmer Press, pp. 46-62.

BOOTH, T. (1981) Demystifying integration, in SWANN, W. (Ed.) *The Practice of Special Education,* Oxford, Blackwell, in association with the Open University Press.

BOOTH, T. (1982) 'Working Towards Integration', *Where,* No. 178, pp. 21-5.

BOOTH, T. (1983) 'Policies Towards the Integration of Mentally Handicapped Children in Education', *Oxford Review of Education,* 9, 3, pp. 255-68.

CASTLES, F.C. (1985) *The Working Class and Welfare: Reflections on the Political Developments of the Welfare State in Australia and New Zealand 1890-1980,* New Zealand, Allen and Unwin.

CASTLES, F.C. and MCKINLAY, R.D. (1979) 'Public Welfare Provision, Scandinavia, and the Sheer Futility of the Sociological Approach to Politics', *British Journal of Political Science,* 9, pp. 157-71.

CODD, J.A. (1988) 'The construction and deconstruction of educational policy documents', *Journal of Education Policy,* 3, 3, p. 235-47.

COMMONWEALTH SCHOOLS COMMISSION (1985) *Report of the Working Party on Special Education on Commonwealth Policy and Directions in Special Education,* Canberra, May.

CULLEY, L. and DEMAINE, J. (1983) 'Social Theory, Social Relations and Education', in WALKER, S. and BARTON, L. (Eds) *Gender, Class and Education,* Lewes, Falmer Press, pp. 161-72.

DEMAINE, J. (1981) *Contemporary Theories in the Sociology of Education,* Basingstoke, Macmillan.

FULCHER, G. (1987) 'The Politics of Integration Policy: its nature and effects', Paper presented at the National Conference of the Australian Association of Special Education, Melbourne, 9-11 October.

FULCHER, G. (1988) 'Integration: Inclusion or Exclusion?' in SLEE, R. (Ed.) *Discipline and Schools: A Curriculum Perspective,* Macmillan Australia.

FULCHER, G. (1988) 'Some Arguments against Professionalism', Paper prepared for the Australian and New Zealand Association of Psychiatry, Psychology and Law workshop, Melbourne, 30 July.

FULCHER, G. (forthcoming) *Disabling Policies? A Comparative Approach to Education Policy and Disability,* Lewes, Falmer Press.

GERRY, M.H. (1985) 'Policy development by state and local education agencies: the context, challenge, and rewards of policy leadership', *RASE,* 6, 3, pp. 9-17.

GERTH, H.H. and WRIGHT MILLS, C. (1970) *From Max Weber: Essays in Sociology,* London, Routledge and Kegan Paul.

GOACHER, B., EVANS, J., WELTON, J., WEDELL, K. and GLASER, D. (1986) *The 1981 Education Act: Policy and Provision for Special Educational Needs,* a Report to the Department of Education and Science, University of London Institute of Education, October.

HANSEN, J. (1982) 'Educational Integration of Handicapped Children, *Child Health,* 1, pp. 156-61.

HANSEN, J. (1984) 'Handicap and Education: the Danish Experience', an Elwyn Morey memorial lecture, Monash University, Melbourne, Australia.

HANSEN, O. (1981) *A Research Project in the Municipal School: Integration of Mentally Retarded,* School Psychology Advisory Service, Hinnerup.

HANSEN, O. (no date: A) 'The Knowledge Seeking Pupil: A model to "trade describe" Special Instruction', School Psychology Advisory Service, Hinnerup, typescript.

HANSEN, O. (no date: B) 'A model of Guidance — Declaration of Special Education', School Psychology Advisory Service, Hinnerup, typescript.

HARGROVE, E.C. *et al.* (1983) 'Regulation and Schools: The Implementation of Equal Opportunity for Handicapped Children', *Peabody Journal of Education* 60, 4, pp. 1-126.

HINDESS, B. (1986) 'Actors and Social Relations' in WARDELL, M.L. and TURNER, S.P. (Eds) *Sociological Theory in Transition,* Boston, Allen and Unwin, pp. 113-26.

HINDESS, B. (1987) *Freedom, Equality and the Market: Arguments on Social Policy,* London, Tavistock Publications.

Integration in Victorian Education (1984) Report of the Ministerial Review of Educational Services for the Disabled (chair M.K. Collins), Melbourne, Government Printer.

JAMROZIK, A. (1988) 'Review of Evers, A., Nowotny, H. and Wintersberger, H. (Eds) *The Changing Face of Welfare,* Aldershot, Hants, Gower Publishing Company, in *SWRC Newsletter,* No. 28, February, pp. 26-7.

KIRP, D. (1983) 'Professionalization as a policy choice: British Special Education in Comparative Perspective', in CHAMBERS, J.C. and HARTMANN, W.T. (Eds) *Special Education Policies, their History, Implementation and Finance,* Philadelphia, Temple University Press, pp. 74-112.

KIRP, D.C. and JENSEN, D.N. (1986) (Eds) *School Days, Rule Days,* Lewes, Falmer Press, pp. 1-17.

LEWIS, J. (1988) Letter to *The Age,* 5 April.

MEHAN, H. (1983) 'The role of language and the language of role', *Language in Society,* 12, pp. 187-211.

MEHAN, H. (1984) 'Institutional decision-making', in ROGOFF, B. and LAVE, J. (Eds) *Everyday Cognition: Its Development in Social Context,* Cambridge, Massachusetts, Harvard University Press.

MEHAN, H., MEIHLS, J.L., HERTWECK, A. and CROWDES, M.S. (1981) 'Identifying handicapped students', in BACHARACH, S.B. (Ed.) *Organizational Behaviour in Schools and School Districts,* New York, Praeger, pp. 381-422.

MINISTRY OF EDUCATION (no date) *Education in Denmark: Educational Normalization for Handicapped Persons,* Special Education Section, Copenhagen.

MINISTRY OF EDUCATION (1986) *Handicapped Students in the Danish Educational System,* A survey prepared for the IX international school psychology colloquium, Copenhagen, Ministry of Education, Special Education Section, August.

MINISTERIAL PAPER NUMBER 1, *Decision Making in Victorian Education,* Melbourne, Government Printer.

OFFE, C. (1984) *Contradictions of the Welfare State,* London, Hutchinson.

PEDERSEN, E.M. (no date: A) 'Integration of Retarded Children in Theory and Practice', typescript.

PEDERSEN, E. (no date: B, post 1982) 'Some statistics on special education', typescript (Consultant to the Ministry of Education).

QUICKE, J. (1986) 'A Case of Paradigmatic Mentality? A reply to Mike Oliver', *British Journal of Sociology of Education,* 7, 1, pp. 81-6.

RIZVI, F., KEMMIS, S., WALKER, R., FISHER, J., and PARKER, Y. (1987) *Dilemmas of Reform: An overview of issues and achievements of the Participation and Equity Program in Victorian Schools 1984-85,* Geelong, Deakin University, February.

SHAPIRO, M.J. (1981) 'Disability and The Politics of Constitutive Rules', in ALBRECHT, G.L. (Ed.) *Cross-National Rehabilitation Policies,* Beverly Hills, California, Sage Publications, pp. 84-96.

SIMON, B. (1985) *Does Education Matter?,* London, Lawrence and Wishart.

STONE, D. (1984) *The Disabled State,* Basingstoke, Macmillan.

SWANN, W. (1985) 'Is the integration of children with special needs happening?: an analysis of recent statistics of pupils in special schools', *Oxford Review of Education,* 11, 1, pp. 3-18.

TOMLINSON, S. (1985) 'The Expansion of Special Education', *Oxford Review of Education,* 11, 2, pp. 157-65.

TOMLINSON, S. (1987) 'Critical Theory and Special Education: "Is s/he a product of cultural reproduction, or is s/he just thick?" ', *CASTME,* 7, 2, pp. 33-41.

TSCHIDERER, N.P. (1986) 'A Study to Identify the Nature of Integration at the Wonthaggi Primary School in 1986', Research paper presented to the Faculty of Special Education, Melbourne College of Advanced Education, October, unpublished.

VICTORIA, MINISTRY OF EDUCATION (Ian Cathie) (1985) Memorandum to Presidents of School Councils, School Principals and Staff Regional Directors of Integration, *Integration in Victorian Schools,* May 20.

VICTORIA, MINISTRY OF EDUCATION (1986) Executive Memorandum No. 34 from the Acting Chief Executive (M.K. Collins) to Principals of Schools, Presidents of School Councils, OICs of Student Services Centres, Teachers-in-charge of Education Support Centres, *Enrolment Support Group Guidelines for Regular Schools,* 13 March.

VICTORIA, MINISTRY OF EDUCATION (1986) B.W. Lamb, Director, Integration Unit, Memorandum to all members Senior Officers Group Integration Committee, 29 April.

VICTORIA, MINISTRY OF EDUCATION (1987) Executive Memorandum No. 144 from General Manager (School Division, M.K. Collins) to Regional Directors of Education, Principals of Schools, Presidents of School Councils, Officers-in-charge of Student Services Centres, Teachers-in-charge of Education Support Centres, *Integration Support Group Procedures for Regular Schools (Formerly Enrolment and Support Group Guidelines),* 17 August.

WARNOCK, M. (1978) *Special Education Needs,* London, HMSO (Chair: M. Warnock).

WARNOCK, M. (1978) *Times Educational Supplement,* 25 May.

WELTON, J. and EVANS, R. (1986) 'The Development and Implementation of Special Education Policy: Where Did the 1981 Act fit in?' *Public Administration,* 64, pp. 209-27.

Acts

Britain Education Act 1981, HMSO.
United States PL 94-142, (1975) The Education for All Handicapped Children Act.

Chapter 2

Contradictions in Education Policy: How Regular Education Teachers in Wisconsin Respond to Normative and Non-Normative Disabilities

Christine E. Sleeter

Public education faces two contradictory tasks: providing a rewarding and fulfilling education fairly to all children, while at the same time meeting the demands of a highly complex and stratified social order. Both tasks receive considerable verbal public support, and both are embodied in education policy. Nowhere are these tasks more clearly at odds than in special education policy. While, on the one hand, special education is widely regarded as a necessary means of providing education to a small minority of children who otherwise would have no formal avenue into society, many also view it as a structure for segregating out of classrooms children who disrupt the order and efficiency with which schools prepare the young for future employment. As Tomlinson (1985) points out,

> Although presented in ideological terms as catering for the 'needs' of pupils, the expansion of special education is the result of rational action on the part of those who control and direct education and training, to restructure the education system to fit the perceived needs of a post-industrial, technologically based society (p. 157).

The contradictory nature of these tasks is absent from much discourse about special education, and from virtually all state and Federal policy statements in the United States. Yet in the act of teaching, classroom teachers must face and attempt to resolve contradictions between being fair and equitable to all students, while at the same time differentiating among them to identify and help to prepare them for different roles in a stratified, technological society.

This chapter will explore how regular education teachers in

Wisconsin respond to different kinds of mainstreamed special education students in their classrooms, and how their responses illuminate the nature of contradictory expectations teachers experience. It will also examine special education policies defining what regular education teachers are supposed to do. I will argue that while the language of state special education policy suggests fairness, efficiency, and rationality, structures of schooling that special education policy does not address limit the flexibility and fairness with which regular education teachers can respond to student diversity.

Disabilities as Social Constructions

Disabilities differ quite considerably from one another. It is useful to distinguish between two different kinds of disability categories: those 'that have an objective, sensory basis (that is, blindness, deafness) . . . [and] those in which differences (that is, learning disabilities, mental retardation) are completely subjectively derived' (Ysseldyke and Algozzine, 1982, p. 43). Tomlinson (1982), making a similar distinction, terms disability categories 'normative' and 'non-normative':

> There can be some normative agreement about the existence of certain categories of handicap, of special need, particularly those which fall into what is currently defined as a medical sphere of competence. Thus blind, deaf, epileptic, physical handicaps, speech defects and severe types of mental handicap could all arguably be normatively agreed upon by most people — professional or lay people, using common-sense but often medical assumptions as well as professional expertise. On the other hand, the categories of feeble-minded, educationally subnormal, maladjusted and disruptive are not, and never will be, normative categories. There are no adequate measuring instruments or agreed criteria in the social world to decide upon these particular categories, whether descriptive or statutory. There can be, and is, legitimate argument between professionals, parents, other interested groups and the general public, over what constitutes these categories (pp. 65-66).

The socially-constructed nature of the categories of learning disabilities, emotional disturbance, and educable mental retardation has been argued quite heatedly, especially recently, as more and more students are being placed in them (see, for example, Carrier, 1986; Kugelmass, 1987; Mehan, Hertweck and Meihls, 1986; Mercer, 1973; Sarason and Doris, 1979; Sigmon, 1987; Sleeter, 1986). Debates surrounding these categories will not be reviewed here, but the fact that they are being carried on is important, because they suggest strongly that normative and non-normative categories cannot simply be lumped together and discussed as if they were conceptually alike.

State Policy and the Role of the Regular Education Teacher

The discourse of state policy ignores such debates, and ignores the possibility that special education categories could be socially constructed, serving particular political and economic interests. Both implicitly and explicitly, legislative policy makes assumptions that deny the ambiguity, political use, and tenuous basis of much of special education. Examples will be provided from Wisconsin State Administrative Code PI 11 (Register, April 1986, no. 364).

One assumption state policies make, as Gerber and Semmel (1984) argue, is that all special education handicapping conditions, including learning disabilities, educable mental retardation, and emotional disturbance, 'like disease processes or biological anomalies, exist *within* students, waiting to be detected and measured' (p. 139). Wisconsin's administrative code explicitly locates disabilities in children. It specifies that 'learning disabilities are primarily attributable to a deficit within the child's learning system' (p. 140), and one criterion of mental retardation is that the child is 'expected to have the condition indefinitely' (p. 137). While the code acknowledges that some children experience failure in school because of conditions outside of themselves, it assumes normative agreement on what constitutes fair measures of success and failure, and deflects debate away from the measures themselves by directing educators to focus on characteristics internal to children.

A second assumption is that the process of identifying who has what condition can be orderly, rational, and precise. Gerber and Semmel (1984) write that, 'it is assumed that technically adequate diagnostic instruments exist . . . and that their reliability is sufficiently high that the likelihood of false positives and false negatives is relatively insignificant', and further, 'that decision-making (concerning both eligibility and placement) reliably reflects assessment data'

(p. 139). Mehan, Hertweck and Meihls agree, noting that 'The federal law governing special education is itself based on the comprehensive version of the rational model of decision-making' (p. 112). Wisconsin's administrative code specifies in great detail steps in the placement process, including who should be on the multidisciplinary team making the diagnosis, what sorts of assessment devices should be used for each handicapping condition, and in what sequence the steps should be taken. It is assumed that if the correct assessment devices are used, and data are gathered and evaluated in the correct manner, children with handicapping conditions located inside themselves can be identified accurately. Absent is any mention of technical as well as ethical inadequacies of assessment devices (see Coles, 1978; Salvia and Ysseldyke, 1981), or acknowledgement of organizational and personal factors built into the placement process that actually strongly shape placement decisions (Mehan, Hertweck and Meihls, 1986; Ysseldyke, 1983).

A third assumption is that the child's needs can be served best by matching him/her with the correct placement option. In other words, once a diagnosis has been made of the child's condition, a rational match can be made between child and program in order to enhance the child's access to a fair education. State code in Wisconsin lists a range of options: regular class placement with diagnostic teacher, self-contained complete program, self-contained modified program, self-contained integrated program, resource room program, itinerant program, and homebound instruction program. What a child's needs are become statements on the Individualized Educational Program (IEP); placement is then the most effective vehicle for meeting those needs. Needs are judged in relationship first to the academic curriculum, then to personal, social, and vocational adjustment to the existing society. Questions concerning a broader conception of human needs, or the extent to which mainstream education meets any child's human needs, are avoided in favour of technical questions involving matching IEP goals with placement options. For example, IEP goals for a child classified as emotionally disturbed would probably involve teaching certain behaviours and mastery of material in the existing curriculum. The fact that the child may not be behaving 'properly' due to boredom with the curriculum or alienation from a regimented school-type setting probably would not be addressed at all.

To insure that regular education teachers are prepared to fulfil their role, the state has delineated a requirement that they complete:

a course or courses consisting of a minimum of 3 semester credits or its equivalent in exceptional education . . . Programs shall provide students with the following knowledge:

(a) Knowledge of exceptional educational need areas as defined by state law and federal law.

(b) Knowledge of the major characteristics of the disability areas in order to recognize their existence in children.

(c) Knowledge of various alternatives for providing the least restrictive environment for children with exceptional educational needs.

(d) Knowledge of methods of teaching children and youth with exceptional educational needs effectively in the regular classroom.

(e) Knowledge of referral systems, multi-disciplinary team responsibilities, and individualized education plan (IEP) processes (Wisconsin Administrative Code PI 3.05, Oct. 1984).

From the perspective of state law, the role of the regular education teacher seems conceptually rather simple: to help identify who among the children assigned to his/her class is a member of a given category, to help get that child properly classified, and should that child continue to spend time in the regular teacher's classroom or return at some later date, to modify his or her instruction as needed to accommodate that child.

The idea that processes embedded in the day-to-day practices of schooling could handicap children is absent from state policy discourse. For example, while the requirement that teachers complete coursework in Exceptional Children specifies that they should learn methods for teaching special education students in the regular classroom, it does not specify that teachers investigate ways in which classroom processes handicap children, such as the expectation that all students read at a given level to learn content. State special education policy implies that regular education instructional processes are fine, but that some children, because of characteristics they have, require something different that may or may not be suitable to the regular classroom. State policy helps assure the regular education teacher that variation among his/her students will thus be limited, facilitating the 'batch-processing' (Cusick, 1973) of twenty-five to thirty students at a time. As Pugach (1987) points out, regular education teachers come to believe that they are unable to teach 'those' kids, and that methodologies for teaching children placed in special education are 'those special education approaches, not mine' (p. 169).

And yet, the regular classroom is recognized in state and federal policy as an option in deciding on the 'least restrictive environment' in which the education of exceptional children is to take place. While policy does not use the word 'mainstreaming', by specifying that they be placed in the 'least restrictive environment', the regular education teacher often assumes responsibility for them after all. We are left with a paradox: to what extent is the regular education program expected to accommodate a wide diversity of children, and to what extent is it expected to sort out those who do not meet its demands? State policy asks for both, and does not acknowledge or address the contradictory nature of these expectations.

What Regular Education Teachers Actually Do

Regular education teachers respond by playing a very active role in referring children for special education. Algozzine, Christenson and Ysseldyke (1982) found 3–6 per cent of school-aged children referred for special education evaluation. About two-thirds of the time, referrals result in placement in special education: 92 per cent of the referred students are evaluated, and 73 per cent of those evaluated are placed in special education. The decision by the regular education teacher to refer a child to special education is one of the most important factors in getting that child into special education. According to Ysseldyke (1983), teachers refer children for special education expecting them to be placed there; they view the students' problems as resulting from the home or within-student deficits rather than inadequate instruction or school problems.

Regular education teachers seem more active in referring students than in modifying their own instruction to accommodate those from special education who have been mainstreamed. Despite being admonished by many special educators to adapt their teaching to mainstreamed students, regular education teachers resist making substantial modifications. For example, Sleeter and Grant (1986), in an ethnographic study of a junior high with mainstreamed students, found some teachers unwilling to take mainstreamed special education students at all; others made only small modifications, such as supplying them with a copy of lecture notes, or allowing tests to be taken orally or giving longer times for taking tests. In a field study of a middle school, Truesdell (1985) found regular education teachers to take only the least disruptive LD students, and to make few modifications to their whole-class instruction strategies to accommodate them. Munson's study (1986-1987), based on interviews with twenty-six regular education teachers, concluded that teachers make the same kinds of small modifications for mainstreamed students that they would make for typical students, but do not make substantial modifications that would restructure instructional tasks. Zigmond, Levin and Laurie (1985) found, based on a survey of 132 secondary teachers, that most teachers used whole-class instruction, disseminating content through lecture and the textbook, and adjusted little more than grading procedures for mainstreamed LD students. About one-fourth of the teachers did not believe LD students should be mainstreamed, and another one-fourth would accept them only under certain conditions.

Thus, regular education teachers appear to straddle the contradiction between teaching all students fairly and equally, and differentiating among them, by helping to supply special education with most of its students, and by making very small modifications to their instruction for those special education students mainstreamed into their classrooms. The question arises: to what extent can regular education teachers be made to accommodate a wider diversity by offering them more teacher education aimed toward this? After all, none of the studies above described the regular education teachers as having had coursework in Mainstreaming or Exceptional Children, and one could wonder whether they would more actively try to accommodate mainstreamed students if they had.

Purpose of Study

In Wisconsin, regular education teachers who were certified in the last few years have all had at least one course in Exceptional Children. To explore in more detail how these regular education teachers respond to mainstreamed special education students, and to explore implications of their responses for education policy, I compared three groups of regular education teachers in Wisconsin:

1) those with no mainstreamed special education students
2) those with mainstreamed students from non-normative categories, and
3) those with students from normative categories.

I expected to find the latter two groups of teachers responding to differences among students a little more than the first group simply because the presence of mainstreamed students would widen the range of differences. I was not sure to what extent I would find differences between the second and third groups. What I found was different from what I had expected, and sheds some light on teacher responses to contradictory expectations embedded in education policy.

Sample and Methodology

The study reported in this paper is from a larger study of graduates of Wisconsin teacher education programs who are currently teaching in Wisconsin. The larger study investigated how teachers are working with race, gender, social class, and disability issues in their classrooms (Sleeter, 1987; in press). A self-report survey questionnaire was mailed to 1552 Wisconsin teachers who had been certified by Wisconsin teacher education programs between 1980 and 1985. A total of 456 surveys were returned: 40 of these were unusable for various reasons (e.g., individual not currently teaching, individual certified before 1980, survey completed improperly). Of the 416 teachers in the final sample for the larger study, 262 were regular education teachers. They constitute the sample for the study reported here. Table 1 summarizes grade level and subject area of the sample, dividing them into three groups based on the composition of their mainstreamed students. Six teachers had mainstreamed students from normative categories only; they are included in the third column, but mentioned separately where relevant.

The questionnaire was developed by myself. Drafts were reviewed by members of the Wisconsin State Human Relations Association, which is made up primarily of professors in Wisconsin teacher education programs. The questionnaire contains ninety-four items. The first twenty-five items ask about the teacher's background and present teaching assignment, preservice education, inservice education, and characteristics of students currently in teacher's classroom. The next forty-six items ask how often teachers do specific things in the areas of curriculum materials, content of lessons, instructional strategies, student-student relationships in the classroom, and other teaching-related concerns. Response choices are: never, less than once per month, once to five times per month, more than once per week, and not applicable. The last twenty-two items ask teachers to rank-order barriers and facilitators to multi-

Table 1: Teaching Area and Student Composition of Sample

Categories of Mainstreamed Students:	none	non-normative	normative and non-normative
Number of Teachers	46	122	94
Teaching Kindergarten	30%	4%	5%
Teaching Elementary	37%	41%	33%
Teaching Secondary	33%	55%	62%
Subject areas			
Art		1	2
Foreign Language	1	5	3
English	2	7	9
Math		14	5
Music	6	8	2
Physical Education	1	1	4
Science		7	9
Social Studies	1	3	3
Other		17	13

cultural education and mainstreaming. All questions are multiple choice; responses were to be marked on an optical scan coding sheet.

Ten items on the questionnaire investigate several teaching behaviours that special educators list as components of successful mainstreaming in the regular classroom. Those that have been suggested in the literature include adapting instructional level to the level of the student, adapting testing procedures, matching teaching strategies to student learning style, adapting instructional materials, modifying grading procedures, teaching metacognitive learning strategies, using small group and individualized instruction, having a consistent behavioural management plan, and promoting positive social relationships with other students (Bender, 1986-1987; Munson, 1986-1987; Salend and Viglianti, 1982). The ten items included on the questionnaire investigated curriculum, instruction, and student-student relationships.

Results

The data were analyzed in two ways, and for both analyses, teachers were divided into three categories: those with no mainstreamed students, those with mainstreamed students from non-normative categories only, and those with mainstreamed students from normative and non-normative categories. First, for each item, the percentage of teachers giving each response was calculated. Figures were drawn to depict teacher responses.

Second, a mean score and chi square were computed for each item, in order to determine statistically significant differences among the groups of teachers. Scoring was as follows: never = 1; less than once per month = 2; one to five times per month = 3; more than once per week = 4; and those marking 'not applicable' were not included. For this analysis, since the grade level distribution of teachers differed among the three groups and could in itself account for differences in results, teachers were further subdivided, with those teaching kindergarten and elementary forming one subgroup, and those teaching junior high and high school forming another.

Curriculum

Three questions investigated curriculum, asking how often teachers use materials that included people with disabilities, teach lessons about people with disabilities or handicapping conditions, and deliberately incorporate students' interests and prior experiences into the curriculum.

Including people with disabilities in the curriculum is not a recommendation one commonly finds in the literature for successful mainstreaming. Yet mainstreaming people with disabilities into the curriculum can be viewed as an important aspect of mainstreaming people into other social institutions. Figures 1 and 2 show teachers' use of materials and lessons about disabled people. As these figures show, differences among the groups of teachers were negligible: neither the presence nor absence of disabled students affected the extent to which most teachers include people with disabilities in the curriculum. The chi square analysis found no statistically significant differences ($p < .05$) among groups on these items. Teachers without mainstreamed students probably reported including people with disabilities in the curriculum a little more frequently than teachers with mainstreamed students because a large proportion were kindergarten and elementary teachers. Lower grade level teachers were a little more likely than secondary level teachers to report using such materials and teaching such lessons. The six teachers with mainstreamed students from normative categories differed from the

Figure 1

Use Materials That Include Disabled People

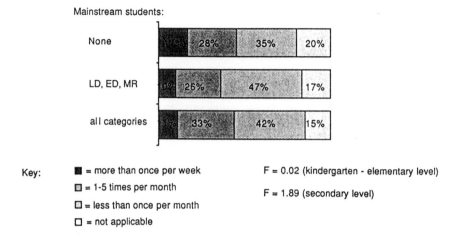

Key:

■ = more than once per week

▨ = 1-5 times per month

▢ = less than once per month

□ = not applicable

F = 0.02 (kindergarten - elementary level)

F = 1.89 (secondary level)

Figure 2

Teach Lessons About Disabled People or Handicapped Conditions

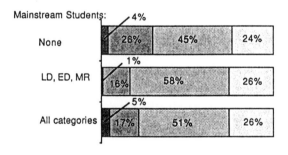

Key:

■ =more than once per week

▨ =1-5 times per month

▢ =less than once per month

□ = not applicable

F = 0.91 (kindergarten, elementary level)

F = 1.11 (secondary level)

others only on the question about materials: 50 per cent of them used materials that include people with disabilities more than once per week.

Figures 1 and 2 show, however, that very few teachers include disabled people in their curriculum very often. Less than half use materials that include people with disabilities and less than three-fourths teach lessons about them more than once per month. About one-fourth consider teaching about them inapplicable. This suggests a widespread acceptance of a curriculum almost devoid of disabled people. Currently in the US, textbook publishers include about one disabled person per text; few teachers appear to go beyond that in their teaching.

Teachers were asked how often they deliberately incorporate students' interests and prior experiences into the curriculum. This question indicates a teacher's responsiveness to the particular students in his/her classroom, and ability to draw on what they know to teach new concepts more effectively. Students from non-normative categories — in particular those classified as mentally retarded and learning disabled — have experienced difficulty learning school knowledge; drawing on students' interests and experiences helps them learn new concepts more effectively. However, as Figure 3 shows, this group of teachers incorporates students' interests and prior experiences *less* frequently than teachers with no mainstreamed students or those with mainstreamed students from both normative and non-normative categories. While most teachers reported incorporating students' interests and prior experiences into the curriculum at least once per week (which is not necessarily very often), almost half of those with students classified as learning disabled, mentally retarded, or emotionally disturbed do so less than once per week. The chi-square analysis did not show statistical significance, although it indicated that this pattern holds more strongly for secondary than elementary level teachers.

Figure 3

Incorporate Student Interest and Prior Experience Into
The Curriculum

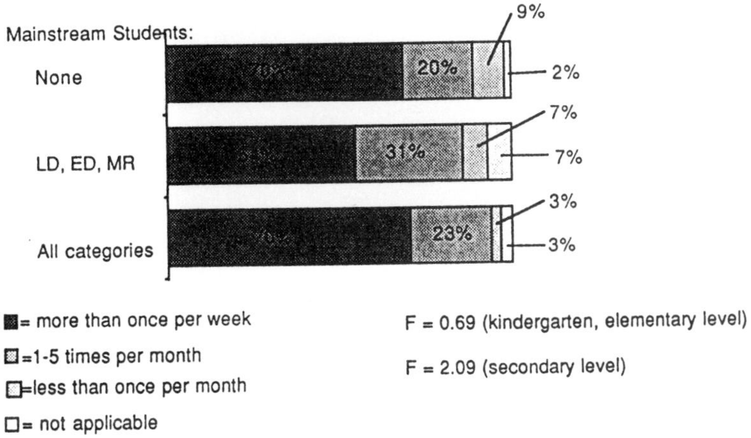

Mainstream Students:

None — 20% / 9% — 2%

LD, ED, MR — 31% / 7% — 7%

All categories — 23% / 3% — 3%

■ = more than once per week
▨ = 1-5 times per month
□ = less than once per month
□ = not applicable

$F = 0.69$ (kindergarten, elementary level)

$F = 2.09$ (secondary level)

Instruction

Four questions investigated teaching strategies, asking how often teachers adapt instruction to student learning styles, adapt to student reading levels, modify testing procedures for mainstreamed students, and reteach concepts for students who did not learn them the first time. As Figures 4, 5, 6 and 7 show, teachers with mainstreamed students from both normative and non-normative categories reported doing all four of these more frequently than teachers with mainstreamed students from non-normative categories only. Chi-square analyses found these relationships statistically significant (p<.05) on all four items for the kindergarten and elementary teachers, although not for the secondary level teachers. However, the secondary level teachers' mean scores were slightly less than those of the elementary level teachers, indicating that they make these modifications a little less often.

Adapting to students' learning styles could mean allowing students to work cooperatively, using visual aids, presenting new information orally rather than in print, and so forth. Such adaptations can be crucially important to virtually any mainstreamed student. While four-fifths of teachers without mainstreamed students, and teachers with mainstreamed students from both kinds of categories reported adapting instruction for students' learning styles at least once per week, only two-thirds of the teachers with mainstreamed students from non-normative categories reported

Figure 4

Adapt Instruction to Students' Learning Styles

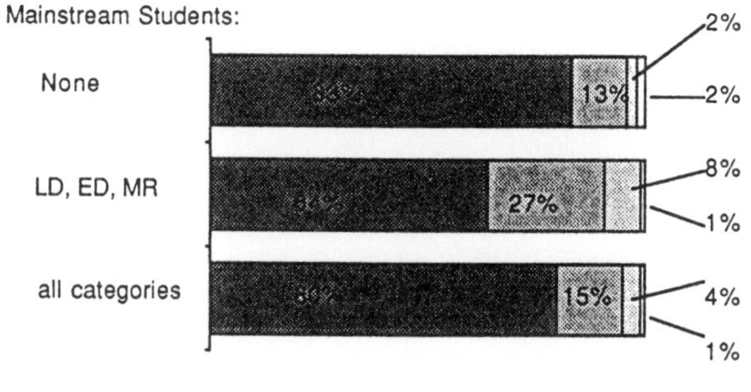

Key: ■ =more than once per week
       ▧ =1-5 times per month
       □ =less than once per month
       □ = not applicable

F = 2.76* (kindergarten, elementary level)

F = 1.98 (secondary level)

*p < .05

doing so that often. All six teachers with mainstreamed students from normative categories only reported adapting for students' learning styles at least once per week.

Fewer teachers reported adapting for student reading levels at least once per week than for students' learning styles, but the discrepency between the three groups follows the same pattern as that for learning styles. In addition, five of the six teachers with mainstreamed students from normative categories only adapt for student reading levels at least once per week, while the sixth marked the question inapplicable.

Teachers can adapt testing procedures in various ways, such as allowing tests to be given orally or extending time limits. As Figure 6 shows, about 55 per cent of both groups of teachers with mainstreamed students reported adapting testing procedures at least once per month; of these, a greater proportion of teachers with students from both normative and non-normative categories reported doing so more than once per week, than teachers with students from non-normative categories only. Most teachers without mainstreamed students marked this item inapplicable; it is unclear why some responded to this question otherwise, unless they were thinking of remedial students in their classes. Of the six teachers with students from normative categories only, three reported adapting testing procedures more than once per week, one reported never adapting them, and two considered the question inapplicable.

Finally, as Figure 7 shows, most teachers reported reteaching

Figure 5

Adapt to Students' Reading Levels

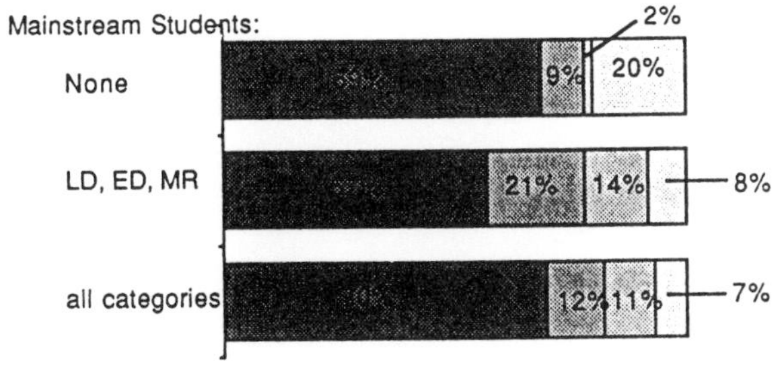

Mainstream Students:

None — 9% | 20% | 2%

LD, ED, MR — 21% | 14% | 8%

all categories — 12% | 11% | 7%

■ =more than once per week
☒ =1-5 times per week
□ =less than once per month
□ =not applicable

$F = 5.48^*$ (kindergarten, elementary level)

$F = 1.05$ (secondary level)

$^*p < .05$

concepts as needed at least once per week, but the proportion was highest among those with no mainstreamed students and lowest among those with mainstreamed students from non-normative categories only. Thus, it appears that teachers with mainstreamed students who are learning disabled, mentally retarded, or emotionally disturbed but *not* physically, visually, or hearing impaired, make instructional modifications for students *less* often than other groups of teachers.

Figure 6

Adapt Testing Procedures for Mainstreamed Students

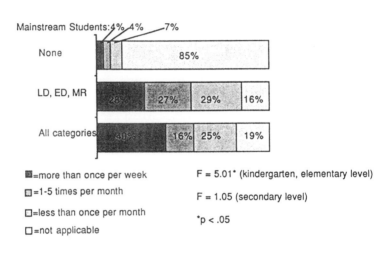

=more than once per week   F = 5.01* (kindergarten, elementary level)

=1-5 times per month   F = 1.05 (secondary level)

=less than once per month   *p < .05

=not applicable

Figure 7

Reteach Concepts as Needed

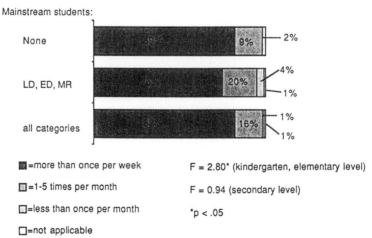

=more than once per week   F = 2.80* (kindergarten, elementary level)

=1-5 times per month   F = 0.94 (secondary level)

=less than once per month   *p < .05

=not applicable

Student-student relationships

Three questions related to improving student-student relationships in the classroom. The first asked the frequency with which teachers deliberately try to reduce social barriers between special education and regular education students. Results are summarized on Figure 7. Half of the teachers without mainstreamed students considered this question inapplicable. It is unclear why one-fourth of those without mainstreamed students indicated doing so at least once per week; they may have been trying to improve relationships between their own students and special education students elsewhere in the school. Of the teachers with mainstreamed students, those with students from both normative and non-normative categories reported trying to improve student-student relationships considerably more frequently than those with students from non-normative categories only. While two-thirds of the former reported doing so at least once per week, only half of the latter reported doing so that often, although these differences were not quite statistically significant. All six teachers with students from normative categories only reported trying to reduce social barriers between special education and regular education students at least once per week.

Teachers were asked how often they use cooperative learning, since this is an effective strategy for improving student-student relationships (Johnson and Johnson, 1986). As Figure 9 shows, over half of each group reported using cooperative learning at least once

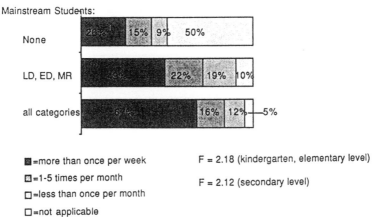

Figure 8

Try to Reduce Social Barriers Between Special Education and
Regular Education Students

Mainstream Students:

None

LD, ED, MR

all categories

■ =more than once per week

▨ =1-5 times per month

□ =less than once per month

□ =not applicable

F = 2.18 (kindergarten, elementary level)

F = 2.12 (secondary level)

per week; a smaller proportion of teachers with students from normative categories only use it that often, than teachers with no mainstreamed students, or students from both kinds of categories. It was surprising to find teachers reporting using cooperative learning so frequently; they may have responded to this question in terms of group work, not necessarily cooperative learning as described in the literature.

Figure 9

Use Cooperative Learning

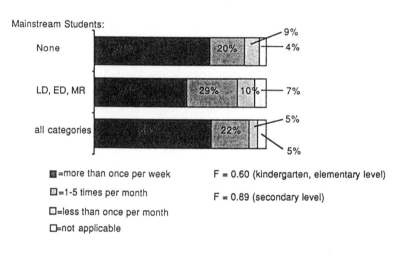

■=more than once per week   F = 0.60 (kindergarten, elementary level)

▨=1-5 times per month   F = 0.89 (secondary level)

□=less than once per month

□=not applicable

Figure 10

Teach Lessons About Stereotyping and Prejudice

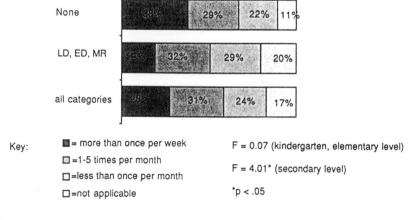

Key: ■= more than once per week   F = 0.07 (kindergarten, elementary level)

         ▨=1-5 times per month   F = 4.01* (secondary level)

         □=less than once per month

         □=not applicable   *p < .05

Finally, teachers were asked how often they teach lessons about stereotyping and prejudice, since teachers frequently use these kinds of lessons to improve student-student relationships (Sleeter and Grant, 1988). As Figure 10 shows, teachers who teach these kinds of lessons most often are those with no mainstreamed students; next, those with students from both normative and non-normative categories; and least often were those with students from non-normative categories only. These differences were almost negligible for kindergarten and elementary level teachers, but they were statistically significant for secondary level teachers. The six teachers with mainstreamed students from normative categories only varied from teaching such lessons less than once per month, to teaching them more than once per week.

Discussion

In general, regular education teachers in Wisconsin who have had coursework in Exceptional Children or Mainstreaming do not respond to mainstreamed students quite as one might expect. They make adaptations for student diversity as frequently, or deal with student social relationships more frequently, when children in their classrooms are physically, visually, or hearing impaired, than when these children are not present. However, they make adaptations *less* frequently when their only mainstreamed students are learning disabled, emotionally disturbed, or retarded, than either teachers without mainstreamed students or teachers with students from normative categories. What we have here is a case of teachers resisting making changes in what they do that could fundamentally alter their curriculum and instruction, but willingly making peripheral changes to accommodate a very small and non-threatening minority of children. State special education policy helps teachers perform their sorting function, while providing an illusion that all children are being provided for fairly. Let us examine specifically what is happening.

Most teachers do not include disabled people in the curriculum very often. The US Department of Education estimates that 12 per cent of public school children are disabled in some way; if so, one could argue that in order for the curriculum to portray people as they are, 12 per cent of the people in the curriculum should be disabled as well. Clearly, that is not the case. If children with disabilities are viewed as somewhat tangential to the main business of schooling, so also people with disabilities are viewed as tangential to school knowledge. They are not entirely absent, but are treated in textbooks as a minority population to add on every now and then. Adding an occasional story about a deaf person or picture of someone in a wheelchair does not transform dominant ideological messages in the curriculum. Seriously treating differences in human learning characteristics, or the life experiences of oppressed minorities would raise major questions about the social order. It probably simply does not occur to most teachers that curricula virtually ignore disabled people and disability issues, since teachers are taught mainly to be transmitters of a fixed curriculum (Apple, 1986), and special education students are assessed relative to the existing curriculum, in the form of standardized tests. State policy does not mention disability and the curriculum, and most teachers do not go beyond the textbook version of how this should be addressed.

The extent to which teachers adapt instruction appears to depend on what categories of disability are in their classrooms. Teachers with mainstreamed students categorized as learning disabled, emotionally disturbed, or mentally retarded incorporate student interest into the curriculum, adapt to student learning styles, adapt to student reading levels, and reteach concepts as needed *less* than the other two groups of teachers, including teachers with no mainstreamed students. The differences between these groups of teachers were more pronounced at the elementary than secondary levels mainly because more elementary teachers reported making more frequent modifications, creating a larger spread between mean scores. Secondary-level teachers adapted to student individual differences less often, regardless of who was in their classroom.

What is it about these three categories that would lead regular education teachers to make fewer modifications in teaching? One possibility is that the separation of teacher education into two distinctly different programs — one for regular educators and one for special educators — leaves regular education teachers feeling unable to teach special education students. Pugach (1987) called this a 'dependence mentality' (p. 170), in which regular education teachers come to believe that they are unprepared in the 'special' methodologies they believe exceptional children require, and that only special education teachers know how to teach these children. Rather than 'looking inward and . . . generating alternative teaching approaches' (p. 170), Pugach argues, regular education teachers believe they must turn the teaching of children designated as disabled over to specialists. This could explain why teachers with mainstreamed students make no more adaptations than teachers without, but it would not explain why teachers with mainstreamed students from non-normative categories make *fewer* adaptations. It is almost as if many teachers use what they already know about adapting to student diversity *less* when faced with those students who got into special education precisely because regular education did not accommodate them well: those classified as learning disabled, mentally retarded, and emotionally disturbed.

Regular education teachers resist making substantial or frequent modifications of instruction for these students because these categories are social constructs that help to legitimate 'business as usual' in regular education classrooms, and regular education teachers help identify who belongs to them. They make most of the referrals, and most students they refer become officially identified as disabled. Let us briefly examine what features of regular education each of these three categories helps to make legitimate.

All three categories can be regarded as statistical creations defining as disabled those who deviate a given amount from the norm on measures designed to rank-order. As such, it is important to look at the measure used to define each category, since that is what is being legitimated. To be classified mentally retarded, a child ranks in the lowest 2 per cent of the population on an IQ test. Essentially IQ tests assess the extent to which one has acquired an 'acceptable' amount of a particular body of information, and can perform abstract and analytic thinking skills in the context of this information, regardless of personal interest. Since the information IQ tests contain has been heavily criticized for its cultural bias, measures of adaptive behaviour have been added, although two commonly-used measures — the AAMD Adaptive Behaviour Scale, Public School Version and the Vineland Social Maturity Scale — are normed such that they tend to narrow the scope of what is considered intelligent behaviour (Salvia and Ysseldyke, 1981). The usefulness of these devices is that they assess the same general pool of knowledge and cognitive skill emphasized in classrooms, such as vocabulary and the ability to perform coding tasks under time limits. When a child is experiencing great difficulty learning what is expected in the classroom, such devices help give legitimacy to the knowledge and kinds of thinking skills in question, rather than the intellectual integrity of the child.

Children classified as emotionally disturbed usually deviate from the norm of passivity in a crowded social space, obedience regardless of personal interest or regard for an authority figure, and adherence to conduct patterns defined by the white middle class as acceptable. The kinds of behaviours teachers tend to identify as symptoms of emotional disturbance are acting-out behaviour, defiance of authority, resentfulness, and lack of interest (Coleman and Gilliam, 1983; Horton, 1973; Rich, 1982). Teacher observation and personal judgment forms a stronger part of the assessment for emotional disturbance than for any other category. The students most likely to be referred are those whose behaviour is distracting or disruptive when teachers are attempting to 'batch process' a group of students.

Children classified as learning disabled deviate mainly on reading level, although relative deficiency in other language and math skills may also be grounds for referral. Several reading and other skills tests are available for giving a precise indication of how a student's skill compares with that of other age-mates or grade level mates. Individual states define exactly how far one must deviate from the norm to be classified as learning disabled. But what is being legitimated is the expectation that children learn to perform relatively complex math and language skills, particularly those involving reading and writing, to a certain degree of proficiency by a certain age. This makes it possible to deliver increasing amounts of information to children via print, and to have them display what they know through writing. Those who cannot keep up present a problem. The category of learning disabilities allows educators to define the problem as the child, rather than the expectation that learning take place primarily through reading. (A high school teacher I recently interviewed told me she teaches a class of low achievers content through film and music quite often; her students learn the content, but she is criticized by some of her collegues for using these media.)

In general, regular education teachers tolerate only a limited amount of deviation from classroom norms due largely to demands placed on them to teach a given body of content in a given amount of time to classrooms of twenty-five to thirty students. Gerber and Semmel (1984) point out that regular education teachers target their instruction to students they consider teachable, focusing on 'modal students . . . in an apparent attempt to reduce the sheer cognitive complexity of planning and instruction associated with broad ranges of student characteristics and abilities.' They go on to point out that, 'in making instructional decisions which ultimately trade increased mean outcomes for the class against reduced achievement variance, teachers behave as if they "prefer" reduced variance' (p. 141).

Experience with special education students can even reduce a regular education teacher's tolerance for them. Shotel, Iano, and McGettigan (1972) found regular education teachers who initially were optimistic about mainstreaming to become frustrated by the consistent low achievement and poor social skills of their educably mentally retarded students. Referring children for special education and refusing to accommodate too much variance presented by those students who have been mainstreamed are important ways teachers can limit the variance in their classrooms and their own subsequent frustration.

Imagine a teacher with several low achievers, most of whom are low in reading. The teacher must mentally determine how much to adapt instruction or materials to these students, and estimate his/her cut-off point beyond which no further modifications will be made and failing children will be referred to special education. Now imagine two of these low achievers are mainstreamed learning disabled students, which the teacher may or may not have wanted. Their presence challenges the teacher's sense of how much variation to accommodate. Should these two students get alternative reading assignments and grading procedures, and if so, why not the other low readers in his/her classroom? After all, these LD students look just as 'normal' as other students who also would benefit from alternative reading assignments. If the teacher makes too many adaptations for them, the other students have a right to expect the same. If the teacher insists on limiting adaptations, his/her workload remains manageable and none of the other students come to expect accommodations for them.

It behoves the regular education teacher to guard and enforce his/her conceptions of normalcy, especially when confronted with 'disabled' students who look normal. It is in the teacher's own interest not to make too many modifications or adaptations for them. Mehan, Hertweck, and Meihls (1986) provide an illuminating account of how teachers described videotapes of students in their classrooms. Depending on how the teacher mentally constructed handicap categories, he/she differentiated among students based on their presumed membership in a category and interpreted their behaviour accordingly. They argued that teachers develop their own understandings of the meanings of non-normative categories based on their own 'expectations for academic performance and norms for appropriate classroom behaviour' (p. 87). The teachers then interpret these handicap categories as 'brute facts' rather than 'institutional facts' (p. 85). Viewing non-normative categories as brute facts, what teachers call into question is whether a particular child should be in the regular classroom, rather than the expectations and norms undergirding the teacher's construction of handicap.

State special education policy helps teachers view non-normative disabilities as brute facts. While state policy delineates steps in the institutional process of designating a child as disabled, it conveys the sense that the institution is simply discovering character-istics of children so that an appropriate treatment can be matched, rather than constructing a way of thinking about student differences.

Regular educators face a somewhat simpler problem when confronted with students who are members of a normative category, although these students display many of the same difficulties with regular education classroom processes. Contrast, for example, a teacher referring a child suspected to be emotionally disturbed with a teacher referring a child suspected as having a visual impairment or cerebral palsy. It is immediately apparent that the latter does not happen very often. Usually a child with a normative disability arrives in the regular education classroom already classified, and usually a physiological basis for the impairment is readily accepted. It is fairly obvious that the child has a disability. The child belongs to a different category of student, and other students as well as teachers can agree fairly readily on this. The regular education teacher rarely helps to decide this, nor need he/she collaborate in a process of reaffirming the legitimacy of the disability classification. Furth-ermore, he/she need not worry about 'lowering standards' for other students, since there is little chance many of them will become members of normative disability categories; if they do, it would be the result of a tragic accident rather than a failure to learn or do what they are told.

This brings us to the importance of a disability being visible or obvious to warrant teacher attention. The data show teachers with mainstreamed students from normative categories more likely than the other groups of teachers to try to improve social relationships between regular and special education students, and to teach lessons about prejudice and stereotyping. Regular education teachers want children with normative disabilities to be accepted, to fit in harmoniously. Their 'obviousness' helps signal or remind the teacher that they may face peer rejection, and for no fault of their own. Students from non-normative categories look like everyone else, although research finds them to be accepted less and often rejected more than their peers (Ballard, Corman, Gottlieb, and Kaufman, 1978; Bruininks, 1978; Bryan and Bryan, 1978; Gottlieb,

Semmel and Veldman, 1978), and they too could use improved social relationships with other students. However, since they look 'normal' and communicate 'normally', it is easier to assume their relationships with their peers are or should be 'normal'. Further, since they threaten a teacher's attempt to limit the range of diversity in the classroom, the teacher is less likely to cater to their social, in addition to academic, needs than he/she is to the needs of a student with a normative disability.

In essence, what we have is the following problem. Schools contain a significant proportion of children who do not fit well into the demands of regular education. To accommodate them, state policy has devised alternative placements for them and procedures for weeding them out of the regular education classroom, leaving its demands intact. As a part of the civil rights struggle, however, the segregation of any child from regular education has been severely questioned. Children with physiological disabilities have a sufficiently acceptable 'excuse' for requiring adaptations that they do not present as much of a dilemma to regular educators as do children without an obvious physiological 'cause' of their difficulties. Regular educators tend to respond to children from non-normative categories by minimizing adaptations in their classrooms. While this response is a source of frustration to these children as well as to many special educators, it is a logical response to the contradiction regular educators face.

State policy makers may be tempted to 'fix' the problem by requiring additional teacher education. However, I would argue that teacher education will not change regular educators' responses substantively. All of the regular education teachers studied here did have some teacher education directed toward mainstreaming special education students. The reasons regular education teachers resist making substantial accommodations for mainstreamed special education students are structured into their work: these include their load of students, the amount of relatively standardized content they are to 'cover', the codified nature of the content, and their role in referring out those who make it excessively difficult to 'batch process' their other students efficiently. Teacher education can give regular educators additional strategies for addressing student diversity, but the extent to which regular education teachers will employ these strategies depends largely on changing what teachers are expected to do.

At a policy level, there is a need to address the contradiction between providing a rewarding and fulfilling education and later life fairly to all citizens, while at the same time fitting people into a highly complex and stratified technological order. Problems reflected in special education and mainstreaming emanate from this larger social issue. While we should support efforts to make life more rewarding and educationally productive for all students at the classroom level, we also need to recognize clearly that actions taken at that level which seem unfair to some kids have a broader social structural basis which state policy only masks.

Acknowledgment

I would like to thank Shepard Siegel and Scott B. Sigmon for their helpful comments on an earlier draft of this paper.

References

ALGOZZINE, B., CHRISTENSON, S. and YSSELDYKE, J.E. (1982) 'Probabilities associated with the referral to placement process', *Teacher Education and Special Education*, 5, pp. 19-23.

APPLE, M.W. (1986) *Teachers and Texts*, New York, Routledge and Kegan Paul.

BALLARD, M., CORMAN, L., GOTTLIEB, J. and KAUFMAN, M.J. (1978) 'Improving the social status of mainstreamed retarded children', *Journal of Educational Psychology*, 69, pp. 605-11.

BENDER, W.N. (1986-1987) 'Effective educational practices in the mainstream setting: Recommended model for the evaluation of mainstream teacher classes', *Journal of Special Education*, 20, pp. 475-87.

BRUININKS, V. (1978) 'Actual and perceived peer status of learning disabled students in mainstreamed programs', *The Journal of Special Education*, 12, pp. 51-8.

BRYAN, T and BRYAN, J. (1978) 'Social interactions of learning disabled children', *Learning Disability Quarterly*, 1, pp. 33-8.

CARRIER, J.G. (1986) *Learning Disability: Social Class and the Construction of Inequality in American Education*, Westport, CT, Greenwood Press.

COLEMAN, M.C. and GILLIAM, J.E. (1983) 'Disturbing behaviors in the classroom: A survey of teacher attitudes', *Journal of Special Education*, 17, pp. 121-9.

COLES, G. (1978) 'The learning-disabilities test battery: Empirical and social issues, *Harvard Educational Review*, 48, pp. 313-40.

CUSICK, P.A. (1973) *Inside High School*, New York, Holt, Rinehart and Winston.

GERBER, M.M. and SEMMEL, M.I. (1984) 'Teacher as imperfect test: Reconceptualizing the referral process', *Educational Psychologist*, 19, p. 137-48.

GOTTLIEB, J., SEMMEL, M.I. and VELDMAN, D.J. (1978) 'Correlates of social status among mainstreamed mentally retarded children', *Journal of Educational Psychology*, 70, pp. 396-405.

JOHNSON, D.W. and JOHNSON, R.T. (1986) 'Mainstreaming and cooperative learning strategies', *Exceptional Children*, 52, pp. 553-61.

KUGELMASS, J.W. (1987) *Behavior, Bias and Handicaps,* New Brunswick, NJ, Transaction Books.

MEHAN, H., HERTWECK, A. and MEIHLS, J.L. (1986) *Handicapping the Handicapped,* Stanford, CA, Stanford University Press.

MERCER, J.R. (1973) *Labeling the Mentally Retarded,* Berkeley, University of California Press.

MUNSON, S.M. (1986-1987) 'Regular education teacher modifications for mainstreamed mildly handicapped students', *Journal of Special Education,* 20, pp. 489-502.

PUGACH, M. (1987) 'The paradox of preparing teachers of learning disabilities', in FRANKLIN, B.M. (Ed.), *Learning Disability: Dissenting Essays,* Lewes, Falmer Press, pp. 163-77.

RICH, H.L. (1982) *Disturbed Students,* Baltimore, MD, University Park Press.

SALEND, S. J. and VIGLIANTI, D. (1982) 'Preparing secondary students for the mainstream', *Teaching Exceptional Children,* 14, pp. 137-40.

SALVIA, J. and YSSELDYKE, J.E. (1981) *Assessment in Special and Remedial Education,* Boston, Houghton Mifflin.

SARASON, S. and DORIS, J. (1979) *Educational Handicap, Public Policy, and Social History,* New York, The Free Press.

SIGMON, S.B. (1987) *Radical Analysis of Special Education,* Lewes, Falmer Press.

SLEETER, C.E. (1986) 'Learning disabilities: The social construction of a special education category', *Exceptional Children,* 53, pp. 46-54.

SLEETER, C.E. (in press) 'Doing multicultural education across the grade levels and subject areas: A case study of Wisconsin', Teaching and Teacher Education.

SLEETER, C.E. (1987) 'Preservice coursework and field experience in multicultural education: Impact on teacher behavior', Unpublished manuscript.

SLEETER, C.E. and GRANT, C.A. (1988) *Making Choices for Multicultural Education,* Columbus, OH, Merrill.

TOMLINSON, S. (1982) *A Sociology of Special Education,* London, Routledge and Kegan Paul.

TOMLINSON, S. (1985) 'The expansion of special education', *Oxford Review of Education,* 11, pp. 157-65.

TRUESDELL, L.A. (1985), 'Making it in the mainstream: Special education student behavior and academic success', Paper presented at the Annual Meeting of the American Educational Research Association, Chicago, April.

WISCONSIN STATE Administrative Code PI 11, Register (April 1986), no. 364.

YSSELDYKE, J.E. (1983), 'Current practices in making psychoeducational decisions about learning disabled students', *Annual Review of Learning Disabilities,* 1, pp. 31-8.

YSSELDYKE, J.E. and ALGOZZINE, B. (1982) *Critical Issues in Special and Remedial Education,* Boston, Houghton Mifflin.

YSSELDYKE, J.E. and ALGOZZINE, B. (1983) 'LD or not LD: That's not the question!' *Journal of Learning Disabilities,* 16, pp. 29-31.

ZIGMOND, N., LEVIN, E. and LAURIE, T.E. (1985) 'Managing the mainstream: An analysis of teacher attitudes and student performance in mainstream high school programs,' *Journal of Learning Disabilities,* 18, pp. 535-41.

Chapter 3

Educational Programmes for Deaf Students: An Inside Perspective on Policy and Practice

Susan Foster

Introduction

In their history of education for deaf people in the United States and Europe, Moores and Kluwin (1986) note that many elements of what educators today call 'mainstreaming,' are not new practices. For example, the earliest residential schools for deaf children were established as day schools. They were usually built in metropolitan areas, thus enabling a proportion of students to live at home. Other deaf children were educated within schools designed to serve primarily non-disabled students (hereafter referred to in this chapter as regular schools), with varied levels of support and success. This period was characterized by optimism for the potential of deaf students (and other people with disabilities) to learn and function successfully within the larger society.

However, this optimism dimmed during the latter part of the nineteenth and early part of the twentieth centuries. During this period, the trend was towards isolating all people with disabilities from the larger society, stemming from the belief that such people were a threat and, if allowed to mingle with non-disabled people, might possibly 'taint' and thus weaken the larger genetic pool (Wolfensberger, 1975; Deutsch, 1949). This period, often referred to as the eugenics period, resulted in the removal of many people with disabilities from the social 'mainstream', and their containment within large segregated facilities situated in isolated rural areas. It was then that residential schools for the deaf were constructed outside of cities, where students were removed from families and the larger populace.

After World War II, the eugenics movement and its accompanying policies began to wane. Parents, professionals, and people with disabilities began to advocate the integration of people with disabilities within mainstream institutions, including the schools. The passage in 1975 of US Public Law 94-142, also known as The Education for All Handicapped Children Act, reflects renewed efforts to support children with disabilities within regular schools. A central premise of this law is that children with disabilities should be educated within the 'least restrictive environment,' described as follows:

> Each public agency shall insure:
> (1) That to the maximum extent appropriate, handicapped children, including children in public or private institutions or other care facilities, are educated with children who are not handicapped, and
> (2) That special classes, separate schooling or other removal of handicapped children from the regular educational environment occurs only when the nature or severity of the handicap is such that education in regular classes with the use of supplementary aids and services cannot be achieved satisfactorily. (Education of the Handicapped Act, Reg. 300.550)

This regulation has generally been interpreted to mean that the regular classroom should be the 'first of several alternatives considered' in developing educational plans for children with disabilities (Stuckless and Castle, 1979). However, there are differences of opinion about whether children with disabilities should first be placed within regular classes and removed to separate programmes only when they demonstrate failure in the initial placement, or placed first within a separate setting if it is felt that they would not thrive in a regular class. These differences of opinion have been articulated through a heated and ongoing debate broadly centered on the distinction between separate and integrated programming and competing interpretations of PL 94-142.

This debate is particularly intense in the area of education of people who are deaf. For example, in their recently published report to the President and the Congress of the United States, The Commission on Education of the Deaf states that 'the least restrictive environment concept has not been appropriately applied by federal, state, and local education agencies for many children who are deaf' (p. 24), arguing that placement in regular classes is often more restrictive than placement in separate programmes. The Commission recommends the 'refocus of the least restrictive concept by emphasizing appropriateness [of the school placement] over least restrictive environment' (p. 27).

Today, educational alternatives for deaf students in the United States generally fall into one of three broad descriptive categories: (1) separate day or residential programmes, (2) separate programmes within regular schools (in which deaf students attend one or more classes separately), and (3) mainstream programmes (in which deaf students attend all classes with hearing peers). Each of these categories reflects differences in expert opinion about how the educational needs of deaf students can best be met. The separate day and residential programmes are for the most part a carry over from the earlier period, when the philosophy was that students with disabilities could best be served in self-contained, separate facilities where specialized resources could be provided while containing costs through an 'economies of scale' approach. Mainstream and separate programmes in regular schools are more closely aligned with the recent trend of serving students with special needs within their local districts. Mainstream programmes are grounded in an interpretation of PL 94-142 to mean placement of the deaf student in all classes with hearing peers; often this involves the provision of individualized support services, including notetakers, interpreters, tutors and resource room. Separate programmes in regular schools include elements of both separate and mainstream programmes by bringing deaf students together from throughout the district to use centralized special services.

Educational policy may be enacted by legislation, but it is implemented through daily practice within the schools. The purpose of this study is to describe day-to-day practice within each of the three categories of educational programme from the perspective of the deaf student. What do they see as advantages and disadvantages of each kind of educational programme? Are there areas of concern to students related to a particular programme type? What are the implications of their perspectives for policy and practice? These are the central questions of this study.

Review of Selected Literature

Given the current debate over educational programming for deaf students, it is not surprising that a great deal of research in the area of education of deaf students within the past ten to fifteen years has focused on evaluation of different kinds of programmes from a variety of perspectives, including those of deaf students, their families, hearing students, and educators. This research has included studies of the impact of both separate and integrated educational programmes on the academic, as well as personal and social achievement of deaf students. For example, research has shown that deaf students in regular school settings tend to have higher levels of academic achievement than their peers in separate classes or programmes (Kluwin and Moores, 1985; Allen and Osborn, 1984). However, these and other studies also raise questions about whether or not integration, *per se,* can account for differences in academic achievement of deaf students. For example, Allen and Osborn (1984) conclude that integration status alone accounts for only a small proportion of the achievement variance. Kluwin and Moores (1985) and Mertens and Kluwin (1986) suggest that other factors not intrinsic to the mainstream class, including exposure to demanding course content and the training of teachers in academic content areas, may account for differences in achievement.

Similarly, research is inconclusive in areas of personal and social development. On the one hand, Reich, Hambleton and, Houldin (1977) found that deaf students who were fully mainstreamed with an itinerant teacher/tutor had higher self-concepts than either deaf students who were mainstreamed without support services or deaf students who attended both separate and mainstream classes. Farrugia and Austin (1980) used the Meadow/Kendall Social-Emotional Inventory for Deaf Students as a measure of self-concept, and found that students aged 10-15 in residential schools had higher self-concepts than their peers in self contained classes. More recently, Evans and Falk (1987) conclude that the separation and congregation of deaf students within schools for the deaf seriously constrains their socialization into the larger society and increases the likelihood that they will substitute the smaller culture of the institution for the larger culture of normally hearing people.

Ladd, Munson, and Miller (1984) studied the frequency and quality of social interaction between deaf adolescents attending secondary-level occupational education classes and their non-handicapped peers. They found that over two years, deaf students developed more frequent and reciprocal social interactions with hearing classmates in school, but not outside of it. In discussing this finding, the authors question whether the lack of out-of-school contact reflected the depth and quality of these relationships or the presence of environmental constraints, such as the distance between students' homes.

Also of concern is the degree to which deaf students are integrated into 'the unwritten curriculum' (Garreston, 1977), that is, extracurricular school activities and informal interactions. Farrugia and Austin (1980) found that deaf students in mainstream programmes have fewer opportunities to engage in these kinds of activities and interactions than do their peers in residential settings.

Research has been conducted in an effort to describe the impact of different school programmes from the perspective of the deaf student. Saur, Layne, Hurley and Opton (1986) found that deaf students experienced spatial, temporal and cultural isolation in the mainstream classroom. Additionally, they learned that classroom integration was dependent upon the interaction skills of both normally-hearing and deaf students, as well as the ability of the deaf student to accept hearing loss and be accepted by classmates. Others (Mertens, in press; Foster, 1989) have found that deaf students from residential programmes describe their social experiences as more positive than students from mainstream programmes. However, there is also evidence that some graduates from residential programmes are less satisfied with the quality of education they received in these schools than are their peers from mainstream programmes (Foster, 1989).

In the wake of these and other studies, researchers and practitioners in the education of people who are deaf have begun to question the degree to which the placement of deaf students in regular schools has resulted in their integration into the total school environment. For example, it is questionable whether deaf students who attend separate classes in regular schools are really integrated since even when these students attend classes with hearing peers, they are most often in non-academic areas such as physical education (Libbey and Pronovost, 1980; Moores and Kluwin, 1986).

Further, there is no guarantee that meaningful interaction will occur when deaf and hearing students are in classes together. As Gresham (1986) and Antia (1982) suggest, placement in the regular class is a necessary but not sufficient prerequisite to integration. Mertens and Kluwin (1986) examined several variables, including social interaction, in an effort to describe differences in the educational process within self-contained and regular classes. It is significant that trained observers recorded no interaction between deaf and hearing high school students in the fifty-one regular class periods they observed, which led the authors to conclude that 'the espoused goal of mainstreaming to encourage interaction between hearing-impaired and normally hearing students was not achieved in the observed classrooms.'

In summary, research has not been able to prove that one kind of educational programme is uniformly better than another. Rather, these studies suggest that there are positive and negative aspects to different kinds of educational programming for deaf students, and that some problems are more challenging and resistant to intervention than others.

Selection and Description of Informants[1]

Potential informants were contacted by letter and asked to participate in an interview study. Following this procedure, interviews were completed with twenty informants (eleven male and nine female). Five informants have one or more siblings with a hearing impairment; of these five, two have deaf parents.

All the informants solicited to participate in the study had previously been enrolled and taken courses in self-contained classes within the college of NTID at RIT and were currently in good academic standing in one of the other eight colleges of RIT[2]. While all the informants needed a certain level of English competency in order to enrol in one of the colleges of RIT, their English and oral-aural skills varied considerably. Descriptive information regarding the communication skills of the sample is displayed in Table 1.

Data regarding the categories of school placements experienced by each informant were collected through the interview, and are self-reported. Not every informant offered clear or complete descriptions of every school programme they had attended. The descriptive data on school placements must, therefore, be interpreted as possibly incomplete and occasionally incorrect. However, informants generally provided sufficient information for location of the school placement within one of the three programme categories described earlier. Only four informants reported attending school(s) within a single category. Twelve informants reported attending school programmes from two categories over the course of their pre-kindergarten through secondary school years and four said they had attended all three kinds of programmes. In total, sixteen informants said they attended a separate day or residential programme, ten said they attended separate classes in regular schools, and fourteen said they attended a mainstream programme for part or all of their education.

Table 1: Ranges and means on selected communication characteristics of the informant group

	Ranges	*Means*
Reading[1]	7.0-12.0	9.4
English language proficiency[2]	57-100	80
Speech intelligibility[3]	1.5-5.0	3.64
Speechreading with sound[4]	0-98	58
Manual reception[5]	1-100	64.5
Pure tone average[6]	37-116	87.3

1 Reading Comprehension Subtest of the California Achievement Tests. Range of possible scores: 5.0-12.0
2 Michigan Test of English Language Proficiency (English Language Institute, University of Michigan, 1977). Range of possible equated scores: 35-100.
3 NTID Rating Scale of Speech Intelligibility (Johnson, 1976). Range of possible scores reflects a continuum from completely unintelligible (1.0) to highly intelligible (5.0) speech.
4 NTID Test of Speechreading with Sound (Johnson, 1976). Scores ranging from 0-100 reflect the percentage of key words understood from Central Institute for the Deaf (CID) everyday sentences received using speechreading and listening.
5 NTID Test of Manual Reception (Johnson, 1976). Scores ranging from 0-100 reflect the percentage of key words understood from CID everyday sentences received through manually encoded English without voice or lip movement.
6 Range of possible dB levels: 0 dB-120 dB (120 dB recorded when no response).

Procedures

Qualitative research methods were used to collect and analyze data. In depth, open-ended interviews were conducted to learn about the school experience from the perspective of the informants. The interviews were semi-structured in that the same topics were covered with every informant. These included experiences within the classroom, participation in extracurricular activities and social life in school. Additionally, informants were asked to describe family relationships and friendships (both within and outside the school environment) during the school years.

Informants' comments were voiced by the informant or an interpreter holding the Comprehensive Skills Certification of the Registry of Interpreters for the Deaf, recorded on audio tape, and transcribed verbatim. Data analysis involved a detailed reading of all interview transcripts with the goal of identifying recurring patterns and themes (Bogdan and Biklen, 1982).

Results

Since most informants had been in school programmes from more than one of the three categories, they were often able to compare programmes, and identify strengths and weaknesses of each. Their comments are organized below by programme category.

Separate day or residential programmes

Sixteen informants said they had attended a separate day or residential programme for part or all of their education. In discussing their school experiences, informants identified strengths of these programmes. First, they said they had many opportunities to make lasting friendships with peers in separate schools, as illustrated in the following quotation:

> *Interviewer:* When you were living at home did you have . . . neighborhood friends?
> *Informant:* Yes. Some. Some hearing and deaf, few of each, but when I lived in the dorms then I made many more friends . . .because living at home, I wasn't much involved with activities. I was with the family. It was hard to meet friends, but in the dorm it was easy to meet because you're involved in activities and there was a lot of deaf people in the dorm.

A second advantage mentioned by informants was the opportunity to participate in extracurricular activities in these programmes. For example:

> In the [school for the deaf] I was involved in many activities . . . Just the same as hearing people do, but I was involved in opportunities like sports . . . many things, many opportunities. I was very interested in being involved in things. I know that if I was in a hearing high school, it would be a little difficult to be involved, so I preferred the deaf school.

Third, several informants described separate day and residential programmes as promoting personal growth by providing opportunities for travel, as well as the development of responsibility and leadership skills. Fourth, informants said they appreciated the level of access to information available in these programmes, including direct communication with teachers, a high level of expressive interaction with peers, career counselling, and the opportunity to learn about deafness and deaf culture. The following quotations are illustrative:

> *Interviewer:* Family [or] residential school, where did you learn the important things?
> *Informant:* My school. Through friends . . . For example, at my school they taught me to be involved in sports, opportunities for field trips, like museums . . . they would explain all of things, in depth. A lot of visual things that we saw . . . the class would to go out to the farm. For example, there are many opportunities to face things. In my family, not so. My father worked. If I was in the mainstream school, I would be going back and forth to home. Where is the opportunity? Residential school offered more opportunities. For example, my friends would go home for the weekend, go to different cities. Go with my friends. Learn something in their city. Learn something about their family. Share. So many opportunities . . . My family, there wasn't a lot of opportunity to talk, really, not much. They would talk, talk, talk, my family would be talking away and I would just sit there.
> *Interviewer:* They did not sign?
> *Informant:* Well, I would have to say, 'What did they say?' And [they would tell me, but] in real simple sentences, not fully, just a simple explanation. I am not interested in that. I am interested in the specifics of what you're saying, I am curious, what did they say. At my school, it is much better there. Any time anybody said anything, it was always in sign, then you knew what they said, to be fair with the deaf, that was nice. I appreciate that . . .

> At the [school for the deaf], I understood everything, I knew what to do all the time because the teachers could sign and explain things more deeply. Lot of information. In junior high school [a separate programme within a regular school], there wasn't enough information. I couldn't hear things. For example, the [school for the deaf] lectured a programme about a college I'd never heard about — NTID. I learned something, but in junior high, they never said anything about colleges for the deaf . . .

On the other hand, informants noted several disadvantages in attending separate day or residential programmes. One drawback is that enrolment in these programmes, especially those involving long commutes to or residence at school, often disrupts normal home and neighbourhood life, including relationships between the deaf student and parents, siblings, and neighbourhood friends. As one person put it, 'I missed . . . coming home on the bus and changing clothes and going out and playing.' Vacations and holidays at home were particularly difficult, since the deaf student was away from school friends. Secondly, some informants expressed the belief that the education they received in separate day or residential programmes is not as good as that received by hearing students or deaf peers attending regular schools. Underlying both these drawbacks is a feeling of fundamental separation — cultural, academic, social and physical — from the mainstream of society, and a concurrent lack of experience with hearing people and knowledge about what life with hearing people is like. Some examples:

Before high school graduation, I had job frustrations with hearing people on the job, really frustrating. Not understanding, writing papers. But later, coming into [college], had to [interact] with hearing people around and do some kind of communicating, lip reading, understanding that a bit. For the first time on my [college] co-op . . . I felt quite ambitious to talk with the hearing, which is different. In high school, I had really been sort of afraid of the hearing and very awkward . . .

I prefer mainstream . . . because it is more educational than my school. For example, my classmates, all of us, there was some slow learners. The teacher would kind of [be] soft and understanding, and explain again, next day, explain it over again, same thing over and over and over again. I prefer something different all the time . . . hearing [classes] at [college], one day you learn something, the next day, it's another topic and you just keep going. If you don't understand, you just go see a tutor. But at the deaf schools, the same thing over and over again. It causes you to get really far behind.

. . . [at the separate school for the deaf] I started to learn sign, started to learn what deafness was like, started to learn my own. One thing was missing, learning to grow independent, learning to be yourself, learning to have an attitude of fight for it and be like the others, not shut away from the world . . .

Over there [at the school for the deaf], you're classified as handicap. Over here [mainstream] you're classified as normal. That's the only way I can explain it.

In the following quotation, an informant who lived at home and attended regular schools, describes the difference between his experience and that of his deaf sibling, who attended a residential school:

Informant: [My deaf brother] went to the deaf school . . . He wanted to come back home, because I guess he saw me being pretty normal. My brother was an oddball because he was being sent away to a school 250 miles away and he stayed down there. He came home for the holidays, so he felt he was losing a family experience, family life. So he decided he wanted to come back home . . .

Interviewer: . . . You said that he was seeing that you were more normal. Can you explain what you meant by 'more normal?'

Informant: OK. I lived at home. I had parents to live with and a sister. I had a house. I came home every day. I had friends in the neighborhood. I went to a school that wasn't too far away from home. I had the home life. My brother had the institute life. He didn't have a family. His family was his friends and his parents were his teachers, or whoever favored him. So, he had a different life.

Another informant describes a dramatic transition which he underwent during his years at the institution. His comment is illustrative of the kinds of trade-offs which deaf students face in selecting school programmes; in this case, the trade is between family life and companionship with school friends:

I started to learn sign [when I] was sent to school, you see. Mother was so worried because it was four hours away. The school was a four hour drive. I was only 7 years old. But then I learned and learned. I was so enthusiastic and I just talked and talked in school. I learned so much. Many children, always have great influence. We learn so much from each other. I was so happy. I would come home and realize that I didn't fit in my family, in some way. I preferred school.

In summary, students who attended separate day and residential programmes sometimes gave up a 'normal, family life' for the companionship and growth they found at school. In the following sections, we turn to the experiences of students who lived at home and attended regular schools, and the kinds of trade-offs they faced in these programmes.

Separate programmes within regular schools

Ten informants reported attending separate programmes within regular schools for part or all of their education. These programmes varied widely; some had as few as ten deaf students enrolled, while others had fifty or more deaf students. In some programmes, the deaf students were taught entirely within separate classes; in others, students were mainstreamed for one or more classes. While these differences sometimes affected informants' descriptions of the advantages and disadvantages of these settings, some central themes were identified. For example, one advantage of these programmes — especially the larger ones — is that deaf students could find with each other opportunities for social interaction and extracurricular activity which might be unavailable in settings in which they were the only deaf person. In the following quotation, an informant describes the differences between the kinds of interactions he enjoyed with peers in and out of class:

> *Informant:* I wasn't much involved with activities involving hearing students. We tended to stay apart . . .
> *Interviewer:* Did you feel that you were accepted by hearing students?
> *Informant:* Oh, yes, in high school, it seemed I was pretty well accepted. And definitely in class I felt accepted. Outside of class . . . I think I was always pretty much accepted. I didn't feel rejected. There were a few hearing people who weren't very understanding, of course, a few . . . mostly I got along fine. Still, there was a little bit of a separation. I think deaf people tend to stay with one another, and hearing people tend to stay with one another . . . occasionally, there'd be a hearing student anxious to come across and hang with us, or a deaf student trying to get involved with hearing students. But [that happened] more occasionally [than frequently.]
> *Interviewer:* Why do you think that . . . separation is occurring?
> *Informant:* I don't know why. I think the deaf feel more comfortable [with each other] . . . Maybe too much talk or

they get fed up with trying to communicate with hearing people. More comfortable in a group with the deaf.

Interviewer: Did you see separation in school and outside?

Informant: Mostly . . . out of class. Within the class, there didn't seem to be that much separation taking place. There was a real mix of interaction.

Interviewer: Did you feel part of the school?

Informant: Yeah, part of the educational programme. I always felt I'd been a part.

Second, the opportunity to enrol in either mainstream or separate classes was seen as an advantage by some informants. In the following story a student describes his sense of achievement when he enrolled in mainstream classes:

> *Informant:* [mainstreaming into hearing classes] I think it was a real exciting experience for me. I remember in seventh grade, I started going to mainstreamed classes. I was really excited because now I was just like the hearing students. It was more of a challenge. I felt better that I'd be up on the same grade level instead of being behind . . . I got a 'B' grade . . . and it gave me hope that I could continue to get along in classes with hearing students . . .

Another informant describes his hesitation to move into a mainstream math class despite encouragement by others; for him, the knowledge that he could return to the separate class if he experienced difficulty provided a 'safety net' which enabled him to take the risk of entering class with hearing students:

> High school was when they really wanted to mainstream the students that were contained in a deaf programme . . . I remember being asked to go to hearing classes whenever they thought I should and I accepted about three quarters of the time and rejected about one quarter of the time. For example, I was never really strong in math and after my first year in a self-contained math classroom, I did very well in algebra. They thought I would be able to handle the hearing class. So they asked me to go to Algebra II in the hearing class and I didn't want to. I told them that math was not my area, even though I did well the year before. I didn't want to go, but they made me. They said, 'Well, just try it, if you don't do well, we'll put you back in the deaf class.' That made me feel a little better, so I went.

A third advantage is that attending separate programmes within hearing schools affords deaf students the opportunity to interact with *both* deaf and hearing peers:

> . . . We had a pretty good relation between the deaf and hearing in our school . . . It was a good experience for me. I learned to get along with both hearing and deaf people.

Informants also identified drawbacks to separate programmes for deaf students within regular schools. For example, a long commute to school on a 'special bus' was often necessary, enhancing some students' sense of difference within the hearing school. The commute also disrupted the normal pace of the school day, often limiting opportunities for informal peer interaction and extracurricular activity. In the following story, a student describes his frustration with the commute to school, and his relief when he was transferred to a school nearer home:

> The only thing that I ever complained about was that I got tired of going to schools that were half an hour away or 45 minutes away in a taxi cab . . . We didn't pay for it, the school programme did, but it was a long distance every day. I hated getting up too early in the morning to get to school when other kids who lived close by could sleep a little longer then get to school in less time, and I was also an athletic person. I liked playing baseball and when I played baseball, it was always a problem of transportation from getting me home to school. So I made it a point to find me a public school that would accept a mainstreamed programme nearby home. When I reached eighth grade, they finally did that. They found a public school that was a mile away and it was wonderful. I walked to school every day. I didn't want to take the school bus because it took an hour to pick up the rest of the kids and get to school, while it took me maybe half an hour to walk that mile, and I'd be at school feeling good. So I even walked to school on rainy days.

Second, informants sometimes expressed dissatisfaction with the quality or level of the instruction in separate classes:

> I was born deaf, went to a special school where deaf were included, special education for deaf students within a public school, through elementary all the way through junior high. Up to junior high there was always one teacher with varying

levels of students, you know, for their learning experience . . .
[I was] kind of 'stuck with them,' because I wasn't that far
behind and others were . . . that made me lose in [that]
atmosphere, because they're learning something that I
already learned before.

Even when informants were placed within mainstream classes, they
sometimes experienced separation from hearing students. In some
cases, this was due to a lack of self-confidence or self-esteem. In
other cases, the deaf student was struggling to separate from a larger
subgroup of deaf peers in an effort to identify with hearing students.
The need to prove oneself to hearing peers was often closely tied to
this separation and efforts to overcome it. Some examples:

I used to join a lot of sports, outrun the boys, and beat them
in sports. I always had to prove myself . . . I had to show them
that I was a person too. I realize that now, I didn't realize it
then. I had [few] friends. I was frustrated and I felt different
from everyone else. When I was in the hearing class, like the
teacher would talk . . . the teacher would have a little group
in a circle and I would sit there with the teacher. The teacher
would talk about something. I never forget one time when
she talked about a farm and what the farm had. The first
thing that hit my mind, she had a picture of a cow. She asked
'What does the cow give?' I felt stupid because I didn't know
the answer . . . I felt really dumb. Some of the kids were
laughing but I got used to it.

. . . There were about 50 deaf students. They weren't all in
mainstream classes. About three quarters of them were in
self-contained deaf classes which were behind. That was their
level. But there were a few deaf students, about one quarter,
who were out in the fully mainstreamed classes, and I think
because they saw those other deaf students and the cultural
differences — the immaturity or whatever — they got
sometimes the wrong idea about deafness. And sometimes
I'd show them that I wasn't like all those other deaf students,
[that] there's a different group, just as there are differences in
hearing students — some are average, below average; some
way above average. It's just the same with deaf. Not all deaf
students are behind. Some are very able to succeed . . . and
some of the hearing students weren't aware about this.

In summary, informants described their participation in separate programmes for deaf students within regular schools as having both advantages and disadvantages. Their comments suggest that this kind of placement contains elements of both the 'best' and 'worst' of separate day or residential schools and fully mainstream programmes.

Mainstream programmes

Fourteen informants had attended mainstream programmes for part of their education. Generally, the advantages and disadvantages they reported were the opposite of those reported for separate programmes for deaf students. For example, one important advantage cited is that mainstream programmes offer a more challenging level of education than do separate programmes. Closely related is the feeling expressed by some students that attendance in a mainstream programme, *even when to do so is difficult or is not the student's own choice,* is valuable because it is symbolic of 'making it' in the hearing world, and provides opportunities for interaction with hearing people. The following examples are illustrative:

> I benefited from going to a mainstreamed school . . . since we're in a hearing world, you kind of have to adapt to the environment around you. And I have noticed that by going to a mainstreamed school . . . I'm learning how to get along with hearing peers, how to get along with hearing people around me, learning how to keep up. It's helped me a lot.

> I prefer the residential school because the deaf, they fit my culture . . . [But] I grew from going to the institute to [mainstream] high school. Most of the deaf haven't had that experience of going through the mainstream and see what it looks like, and I've had that. So that's an advantage for me.

A third advantage is that the routines of home and family life are best preserved by attending mainstream schools, since students can ride the bus or walk to local schools, come home and play with neighbourhood friends, and participate in family activities. While some informants readily admitted that they were not completely assimilated into their family due to communication barriers, they appreciated the *opportunity* to develop family ties.

The drawbacks identified by informants with their experiences in mainstream programmes often reflected the absence of advantages enjoyed in separate programmes for deaf students. For example, they frequently described their participation in extracurricular activities as limited:

> *Informant:* In the seventh and eighth grade, I was a member of . . . a sports athletics association . . . it's only for girls . . . like bowling in the fall, and winter I think it was basketball, in spring volleyball. I was only interested in bowling. I tried basketball — yuck. It was very hard to communicate. So I don't know how, so forget it. Just with the bowling, seventh and eighth grade. Then ninth grade and tenth, home economics club. I enjoyed that, but there wasn't much activity there, so I stopped after tenth grade. Eleventh and twelfth grades, nothing . . . At that time I had just given up. Just did things at home.
> *Interviewer:* When you said 'give up,' what do you mean? . . .
> *Informant:* Because hearing people weren't interested in me. No one would talk to me, so I just gave up . . . I just had to sit there and watch . . . They'd just tell me what to do, and that's all. I know why, because we had a hard time . . . when we were talking.

Second, informants' descriptions of their experiences in mainstream classes suggest that these settings vary widely in degree of accessibility and support available to students; for example, some informants reported that they had interpreters, notetakers, and tutors, while others said they were essentially on their own. This range of possible environments was both a weakness and strength of mainstream programmes. The disadvantage lies in the unpredictability and variance across mainstream settings — deaf students can find themselves in very supportive situations or totally without support. This variability also can be turned to the advantage of the deaf student, since even a bad situation can be improved with added support, and students who are dissatisfied with one setting might arrange for transfer to another school within the district.

However, having support services does not guarantee successful integration into mainstream class activities. For example, one informant reported difficulty adjusting to an interpreter in class after years of being without this support. Another said he used his time in the resource room for homework, since the resource room teacher lacked the skill in advanced content areas to assist him in his studies. Moreover, informants in mainstream programmes frequently experienced constraints on participation in class activities, including a lack of complete information, limited involvement in class discussions, and a sense similar to that expressed by informants in separate programmes within regular schools of needing to 'prove oneself' to hearing teachers and classmates. Some examples:

> [In class discussions] I always said 'I don't know' because I didn't want to participate and be embarrassed if I gave the wrong answer . . . So they just gave up on me 'cause I was afraid to give the wrong answer. I didn't want the hearing people to think I was stupid. Now I understand. It doesn't bother me anymore. But in high school, I was real embarrassed because of the peer pressure . . .

> . . . that high school, unfortunately, was not experienced with having deaf students before. So the teachers were scared. They didn't know what to do. For example, one application, they'd give something to everybody and they wouldn't give it to me. They probably thought it was too tough for me. I'd say, 'No. I want to be like with them [hearing classmates]. Come on, give me things.' So [they'd] let me try it and found that I could do very well, just like the others.

The most serious drawback of mainstream programmes involved social isolation, that is, the lack of close friendships and social interaction with hearing classmates. While some informants said they had close hearing friends at school, more said they were lonely or described interactions and relationships with hearing peers as casual and short term, as opposed to closer and sustained relationships with deaf friends. In the following quotation, an informant describes her separation from hearing peers, and the companionship she found with the only other deaf student in her school. While one cannot help but be grateful that she was not completely alone, it should also be noted that being limited to one friend for such a long period of time almost certainly constrains social and personal growth:

> *Informant:* In high school, growing up, most of the time I stayed home. I was very quiet and didn't talk much — just simple things . . . I don't talk with hearing people much because they're afraid of me . . . They don't know how to communicate with me or they're embarrassed. A few friends talk from Brownies, Girl Scouts, the same people having been with me at school, and that's all. Also, in high school, it was worse. [I] didn't talk with hearing people much at all, and

I realize its because my speech was really bad . . . that's why
. . . My deaf friend — the two of us — we were the only deaf
in hearing school. Most of the time, I'd go over to her house
or she'd go over to mine, or we'd go together to the football
game, movies. Most of the time I spend with her. When I was
[in] fourth through sixth grade, [I had] some hearing friends.
We went out together to the movies or to eat. Until late
junior high school, then no one was interested in me.
[During that time] I felt bad. I wished I had good speech and
could talk, but I accepted it because I had my friend who was
deaf.

As noted earlier, choosing between different kinds of school
programmes often involves giving up one opportunity or experience
in order to gain another. The following story is illustrative:

There was one time in my life I was so depressed because I
had no friends. I was about 16 or 17 . . . My mother actually
came to me and said '. . . if you really want to, I'll let you go
. . . to the school for the deaf.' I thought about it for a while,
but I said 'No'. I didn't want to. Why? Because I have friends
from that deaf school, and I could tell just by talking with
them that I knew more than they did, and I felt if I went, I'd
be very much out of place 'cause every deaf person of my age
that I've met and talked with didn't seem to be knowledgeable. They still talked pretty low . . . With those people, it was
like down here. I didn't look down on them, but that's how
I've always felt . . . I think a lot of it has to do with the kind of
education. I really can't say 'cause I've never visited a deaf
school myself, but I've noticed that the wavelength of talking
with people from regular public mainstreamed schools seems
to be a little higher than people from deaf schools . . . So I
explained to my mother and she said, 'Well, that's your
decision. You want to remain in [mainstream] high school.' I
knew that by remaining in [the mainstream] high school I
would still be depressed from time to time. I also knew that in
the long run, I would benefit more from it than if I went to a
deaf school and increase my social life and decrease my
education . . .

However, while deaf students in separate programmes may have had
more opportunities to develop relationships with deaf peers than did
those in the educational mainstream, it cannot be assumed that

mainstream students were without close friends. Rather, they were forced to seek friends outside the school environment. For those who had attended separate programmes for deaf students in the past, this often involved the maintenance of already established relationships, as in the following example:

Interviewer: All of your friends from the residential school, was it possible for you to maintain friendships with them, or were you all spread out?

Informant: Yes, yes. I maintained the friendships — a few, like three or four go out on the weekends, tell our problems to each other, our feelings about high school, our feelings about being overwhelmed. Many stories, so we share and that made me feel better. I felt like I wasn't the only one. We shared often. We'd go out and have beer and communicate and understand better. That helps me to do better in [the mainstream] high school.

Interviewer: Can you share one story with me . . .?

Informant: Oh, [we talk about things like how] it was hard to communicate with hearing people, hard to maintain good grades in high school . . . it was really the same problem(s) all the time . . .

Interviewer: You were saying [earlier in interview] that in the . . . [mainstream] school, it was hard for you to have real in depth communication with the hearing students. In depth with the friends from the institute is possible . . .

Informant: Right.

Interviewer: In depth means what?

Informant: Well, you can tell personal things, like talk about problems at school, problems with family. You can tell the deaf, but the hearing will just be pissed off or lose those friends in high school. I didn't want that, so I have to keep it in. With the deaf, they understand the problems. No problem, go ahead. The friendship continues. Keep trying and go on. But the hearing — I don't want to be labeled as deaf and say stupid things. I have to just keep going and show that I can do good things well like sports.

Others found deaf friends through community organizations, including social clubs and church. In the following story, the individual who earlier spoke of his decision to remain in a mainstream programme despite his lack of school friends recalls his initial reluctance to associate with the deaf people at his church, and his gradual movement towards them:

> *Interviewer:* You said that you were really involved in the church, and that you had deaf friends there. Tell me about those friendships.
>
> *Informant:* The church that I went to . . . well, this is a very interesting part. I was raised oral, and I'd never heard or understood sign language or the purpose of sign language. When my family joined this church, my parents tried to encourage me to get involved with the deaf group. My parents knew the problems that I was having making friends [at school]. But at that time, I was not ready to join or get involved with the deaf group that was obviously different than I was. Those people were signing, and I was deaf-oral, and proud of it. Proud of being able to speak. For about one year, I continued to go to regular Sunday School class, regular kids of my own age, trying to make friends. I had a little better success making friends with those people in church because in a church environment, you're supposed to be friendly, you know. I had a little more success, but still it was never a really strong relationship. So for the first year when we were members, gradually I started to go over to the deaf department, kind of just watch. Many of the deaf people moved their mouth while they signed so it was very easy for me to pick up 'cause all I had to do was look at their lips. I didn't need the sign. I was 13 years old at that time. So I'd just watch the conversation. From that time on, I started to pick up sign language really fast. By the end of the first year, I had completely dropped going to the hearing regular Sunday School, I went to the deaf church, got involved . . . in time, going to church and being with those people became my favorite day of the week — better than going to school Monday through Friday. Better than Saturday when there's nothing to do. I'd really look forward every day to going to church on Sunday mornings just to be with deaf people.

In summary, many of the advantages and drawbacks of mainstream programmes are reversals of the perceived strengths and weaknesses of separate programmes. These results suggest that students often found themselves giving up one kind of experience in order to gain another. In the following section, the implications of these findings for educational practice and policy are discussed.

Discussion

In reviewing the findings, two points can be made. First, informants' comparisons of different kinds of school programmes involved a process of 'trading options,' in which one kind of advantage must be given up in order to gain another. For example, mainstream settings were perceived as having a better level of education than separate residential programmes, while the latter offered more opportunities for peer interaction and friendship. In the same vein, a loss of family life in exchange for personal growth was a consideration in the selection of residential over mainstream programmes. Separate day programmes within regular schools are a form of compromise, in that students in these programmes could enrol in both separate and mainstream classes, and daily routines of home and family life were strained but not missed entirely.

Second, the search for companionship transcended school placement. All young people seek companionship with peers, and the students in this study were no different. They wanted friends, were frustrated when their efforts to make friends were unsuccessful, and cherished those relationships which flourished. Informants within all three kinds of placements found friends. However, informants described the task of finding and sustaining friendships in mainstream school environments as generally more difficult and frustrating than in separate programmes; as a result, they sometimes turned to deaf peers from past school placements or other institutions, such as churches and social clubs. The biggest difference between the experiences of informants in separate programmes and those in the mainstream involved the level of determination, patience, and creativity required to find and establish friendships.

There are limitations to this study. The sample interviewed is small and reflects the perspectives of a select group of severely to profoundly deaf college students. Moreover, informants in this study are part of the first wave of students to experience the impact of PL 94-142. Over time, the kinks in implementation of this law may be smoothed out. As a result, younger deaf students are more likely to spend their entire educational careers within mainstream programmes and enjoy more and improved support services. Interviews with students who are younger, have a mild or moderate hearing loss, and/or have not gone on to college are recommended.

Implications for policy and practice

As noted in the introduction to this paper, Public Law 94-142 calls for education of children with disabilities in 'the least restrictive environment.' This concept has been interpreted differently by different groups and as a result has been used to support placements in a wide variety of programmes ranging from residential institutions to regular classes. Each interpretation rests on a different under-standing of what the word 'restrictive' refers to; does it mean restrictions on home life, personal development, academic growth, individual freedom, or all of these? The findings of this study have at least three significant implications for educational policy and practice for deaf people, especially as regards interpretations of the concept of 'least restrictive environment.'

The first has to do with the idea of 'trading options.'[3] While there will always be trade offs between different educational models, the fundamental trades described by the informants in this study cannot be justified. All students should have the opportunity for academic *and* personal/social development to the fullest extent possible; nobody should have to give up one to get the other. Similarly, no student should have to leave home in order to receive a full and appropriate education. However, these are the types of dilemmas faced by the informants in this study. Their experiences demand an evaluation of the educational alternatives currently available to deaf students in the United States in light of the concept of 'least restrictive environment.'

The experiences of informants suggest that, rather than provid-ing educational alternatives to deaf students, school systems offer a series of incomplete options, each of which is restrictive in a different way. Informants described social and personal develop-ment in mainstream programmes as restricted. The development of close family ties and familiarity with the norms and values of the larger hearing society were often restricted by attendance in residential programmes. Enrolment in separate programmes within regular schools restricts the deaf student's sense of belonging and normalcy by placing him or her constantly on the 'fringe' of the mainstream school environment, a subgroup always apart. The informants in this study were all successfully enrolled in college. It is not clear whether they were successful in spite or because of their educational experiences. It is clear that they paid a price for success, regardless of school placement.

Second, the social isolation experienced by informants in

mainstream settings suggests that the concept of total educational integration, *as it is currently practiced,* may be failing to meet the needs of deaf students, and possibly of students with other kinds of disabilities. While this is a serious concern for educators of people who are deaf, neither the problem nor solution lies with them, or even with the educational system as a whole. Rather, the basis for the social isolation and sense of failure expressed by informants has its roots in the values of American society. Until there is a greater tolerance of and appreciation for individual differences, it will be impossible to change in any important way the essentially negative experiences of many students with disabilities in mainstream settings, including those of students who are deaf. Moreover, until these broader changes in social values do occur, deaf students who attend mainstream school programmes must be provided opportunities to meet and interact with other deaf people. Efforts to provide these opportunities should not be limited to the school environment, and may include the development and/or use of existing community resources.

Finally, it is suggested that deaf people can play an important role in describing and evaluating educational programmes and other services. They should be viewed as partners to educational planners and practitioners, and encouraged to become architects of their own lives through participation in the design, implementation and evaluation of the programmes and services they use.

Notes

1 The term 'informants' is used here in the sense of 'a source of information,' as described by Spradley (1979) in his discussion of research participants

2 NTID at RIT was established by Public Law 89-36 in 1965 as part of a national effort to enhance educational, social, and employment opportunities for deaf persons. NTID students can attend separate classes for deaf students within the college of NTID or register in 'mainstream' classes with hearing peers within one of the other eight colleges of RIT. In order for a student to be considered for enrolment at NTID, he or she must be severely to profoundly hearing-impaired (70 dB HL or greater in the better ear). The average grade level achievement for students entering NTID is about eighth grade, which places NTID students in the top ten per cent nationally of deaf secondary school students (Trybus and Karchmer, 1977).

3 See Foster (forthcoming) for an earlier articulation of this concept.

References

ANTIA, S.D. (1982) 'Social interaction of partially mainstreamed hearing-impaired children', *American Annals of the Deaf*, 127, 1, pp. 18–25.

BOGDAN, R. and BIKLEN, S. (1982) *Qualitative Research for Education: An Introduction to Theory and Methods*, Boston, Allyn and Bacon, Inc.

DEUTSCH, A. (1949) *The Mentally Ill in America: A History of their Care and Treatment from Colonial Times*, New York, Colombia University Press.

EDUCATION of the HANDICAPPED ACT, Regulation 300.550, Education of the Handicapped Law Report, Supplement 205, November 22, 1987.

EVANS, D. and FALK, W. (1986) *Learning to be Deaf*, Berlin, Mouton de Gruyter.

FARRUGIA, D. and AUSTIN, G. (1980) 'A study of social emotional adjustment patterns of hearing impaired students in different educational settings', *American Annals of the Deaf*, 125, 5, pp. 535–41.

FOSTER, S. (1989) 'Reflections of a group of deaf adults on their experiences in mainstream and residential school programs in the United States', *Disability, Handicap, and Society*. 4, 1, pp. 37–56.

GARRESTON, M. (1977) 'The residential school', *The Deaf American*, 29, pp. 19–22.

GRESHAM, F. (1986) 'Strategies for enhancing the social outcomes of mainstreaming: a necessary ingredient for success', in MEISEL, C.J. (Ed.) *Mainstreaming Handicapped Children: Outcomes, Controversies, and New Directions*, Hillsdale, NJ, Lawrence Erlbaum Associates, pp. 193–218.

JOHNSON, D.D. (1976) 'Communication characteristics of a young deaf adult population: techniques for evaluating their communications skills', *American Annals of the Deaf*, 121, 4, pp. 409–24.

KLUWIN, T. and MOORES, D. (1985) 'The effects of integration on the mathematics achievement of hearing impaired adolescents', *Exceptional Children*, 52, 2, pp. 153–60.

LADD, G., MUNSON, H. and MILLER, J. (1984) 'Social integration of deaf adolescents in secondary-level mainstreamed programs', *Exceptional Children*, 50, 5, pp. 420–8.

LIBBEY, S. and PRONOVOST, W. (1980) 'Communication practices of mainstreamed hearing impaired adolescents,' *Volta Review*, 82, 4, pp. 197–213.

MERTENS, D. (1989) 'Social experiences of hearing-impaired high school youth', *American Annals of the Deaf.*

MERTENS, D. and KLUWIN, T. (1986) 'Academic and social interaction for hearing-impaired high school students', Paper presented at the 1986 meeting of the American Educational Research Association, San Francisco, CA.

Michigan Test of English Language Proficiency (1977) English Language Institute, University of Michigan, Ann Arbor.

MOORES, D.F. and KLUWIN, T.N. (1986) 'Issues in school placement', in LUTERMAN, D. (Ed.) *Deafness in Perspective*, San Diego, College-Hill Press.

REICH, C., HAMBLETON, D. and HOULDIN, B. (1977) 'The integration of hearing-impaired children in regular classrooms', *American Annals of the Deaf,* 122, 6, pp. 534-43.

SAUR, R., LAYNE, C., HURLEY, E. and OPTON, K. (1986) 'Dimensions of mainstreaming', *American Annals of the Deaf,* 131, 5, pp. 325-9.

SPRADLEY, J.P. (1979) *The Ethnographic Interview,* New York, Holt, Rinehart and Winston.

STUCKLESS, E.R. and CASTLE, W. (1979) 'The law and its implications for mainstreaming', in BISHOP, M. (Ed.) *Mainstreaming: Practical Ideas for Educating Hearing-Impaired Students,* Washington, D.C., The Alexander Graham Bell Association for the Deaf, Inc., pp. 15-32.

TIEGS, E. and CLARK, W. (1963) *California Reading Tests,* California Test Bureau.

Toward Equality: Education of the Deaf, a report of The Commission on Education of the Deaf to the President and the Congress of the United States, Washington, D.C., U.S. Government Printing Office, February, 1988.

TRYBUS, R. and KARCHMER, M. (1977) 'School achievement scores of hearing-impaired children: National data on achievement status and growth patterns', *American Annals of the Deaf,* 122, 2, pp. 62-9.

WOLFENSBERGER, W. (1975) *The Origin and Nature of Our Institutional Models,* Syracuse, NY, Human Policy Press.

The research reported in this document was produced at the National Technical Institute for the Deaf in the course of an agreement between Rochester Institute of Technology and the US Department of Education.

Chapter 4

The Special Educational Needs of Teachers

David Galloway

Introduction

This chapter argues that the needs of children and of teachers are interlinked, and that the relationship between them is seen most starkly in the concept of special educational needs. This concept may be analyzed both from a social policy perspective and from a philosophical one. Either perspective requires consideration of the political beliefs and values on which educational policy is constructed. While the rhetoric of special educational needs gives prominence to the needs of the child, this seldom withstands close inspection. Recent legislation in Britain reflects the belief of members of government about the faults in the current education system. The proposals in this legislation reflect politicians' views about the sort of education system that the country needs. Both the beliefs of government ministers about what is wrong with the system, for example, that it creates widespread under-achievement, especially amongst less able pupils, and the values they wish to develop, for example a commitment to hard work, free enterprise and competition, profoundly affect the provision made for children with special educational needs.

Special Educational Needs: A Social Policy Perspective

The 1944 Education Act created categories of handicapped children. The two most numerous were 'educationally sub-normal' and 'maladjusted'. Once a child had been 'ascertained' as belonging to a category, the local education authority was required to provide appropriate special schooling. Identification of handicap was thus linked, quite explicitly, to service delivery. The 1981 Education Act abolished the categories of handicap, and introduced the concept of special educational needs. Nevertheless, the new concept remained as firmly linked to service delivery as the categories it replaced.

At one level, this is both inevitable and desirable. There is no point in saying a child has special needs unless you intend to do something about them. It is when we consider what may be meant by special needs and the range of possible interventions that problems become apparent.

In a sharp critique, Tutt (1985) argued that the concept of special educational need envisaged in the Warnock Report (DES 1978) and in the 1981 Education Act was inappropriate, inadequate and detrimental. It was inappropriate on the grounds that it focused professional attention on the child, with a corresponding neglect of the context in which the child's difficulties occurred. While this might not be the intention behind the formal assessment procedures presented in the Act, they had certainly not helped professionals to examine ways in which the curriculum and teaching process might have contributed to the child's needs. Rather, they had encouraged a deficit model in which professionals sought problems 'in' the child and/or the family.

The inadequacy of the concept of special need, according to Tutt, lay in the lack of professional agreement on the scope and range of needs. Social workers frequently disagree on whether or not care orders would be appropriate (Gelsthorpe, 1984) and there was no reason to believe that agreement between educational psychologists would be any higher. The lack of agreed criteria for defining special needs meant that the way a child's needs were defined was largely a matter of chance, depending more on the educational psychologist concerned than on any objective criteria.

Finally, the concept of need was detrimental to childrens' interests because: 'the lack of definitional boundaries . . . means that the 'net' of formal control systems can be extended without challenge' (Tutt, 1985, p. 31). Tutt cites a 14 year old boy who was caught stealing a ginger cake worth 42p. The theft occurred because the boy had been 'dared' by bullies at school to prove he was not a coward. When his mother heard about this she kept him at home in the belief that continued bullying would lead him deeper into trouble. When the boy was charged with theft and appeared in court, social inquiry and school reports cited poor school attendance condoned by the mother, and as a result the magistrates made a care order.

Again, it would be naive to believe that similarly far reaching decisions are never made on similarly idiosyncratic grounds in the education system. Currently, one LEA (Local Education Authority) is reported to be planning a 'study skills centre' as a way of dealing with the 'underachievement' of Afro-Caribbean pupils. How removal *from* the schools will help these pupils to achieve success *within* the school curriculum is not clear.

Special Educational Needs: A Philosophical Perspective

Logically, we cannot need something unless there is some sense in which we also want it. Even if I say that I need to go to the dentist, but do not want to, the fact that I 'need' dental treatment implies that I want to be free from the discomfort of toothache. It does not follow, however, that when children have special educational needs they want treatment. The reason, of course, is that children seldom identify their own special needs. These needs are identified by professionals, usually teachers or educational psychologists. Moreover, as Simmons (1986) has demonstrated, children are often decidedly unenthusiastic about the treatment offered even if they agree that they need extra help.

In an ideal world, description of a child's special educational needs might be based on comprehensive assessment, using objective techniques of known reliability. In the real world this is not and cannot be the case. The reason is that a teacher's decision that a child has special needs may be motivated primarily by concern about the child's effect on the progress or behaviour of other children in the class. As far as it goes, this is perfectly reasonable. It is also reasonable for a teacher to request help, perhaps in the form of the child's removal to a special school or class, because the child's progress or behaviour is adversely affecting the teacher's self-image and mental health.

There is precious little evidence that special educational provision in special schools or classes, or even in withdrawal groups within the school, has long-term benefits for the children selected to receive it. Indeed, the evidence from numerous studies suggests that children with moderate learning difficulties actually make less progress when transferred out of the mainstream (see Galloway and Goodwin, 1987). Teachers, then, may benefit from a child's removal, but there is little evidence to support the view that special provision will meet the *child's* needs.

Recognising a teacher's need for support, guidance and professional development is clearly not just morally acceptable but necessary. The problem occurs when the teacher's needs and the child's needs conflict. Nevertheless it is clear that if a child's classroom progress or behaviour appears unacceptable, whether to the teacher or to anyone else, then this must logically have implications for what, and how, the child is taught, in other words for the teacher. Saying that the child has special needs diverts attention from the teacher's need. More crudely, it implicitly blames the child for the problem the teacher is experiencing.

This does not, of course, imply that no children have special needs. That would be absurd. It does, however, imply that a child's special needs cannot usefully be seen in isolation from those of her or his teacher.

Unfortunately, though, the concept of special educational need is still more complicated. As soon as we accept that children's special needs are inextricably tied up with those of their teachers, we have to ask who defines the needs of teachers. This question leads us into the political arena.

The Special Needs of Teachers: A Political Analysis

The Warnock Report concluded that up to 20 per cent of children would have special educational needs at some stage in their school career. The political nature of this conclusion is not always appreciated. It implied that teachers should reasonably be expected to teach around 80 per cent of their pupils without additional resources or special help. For the remaining 20 per cent they might reasonably expect additional support over and above what was normally available in their work with the 80 per cent majority. Naturally, this had implications for resources.

In passing, it is worth noting that the concept of special needs in the Warnock Report is logically independent of the children's educational progress, and is consequently self-perpetuating. The reason is that raising *overall* standards does nothing to reduce inequality. The gap between the highest and the lowest attainers in the most successful London schools was as wide as in the least successful (Rutter *et al*, 1979). Even if the 20 per cent of pupils with special needs were the *only* pupils whose attainments improved over a given period, it would still be possible to identify an arbitrary number of pupils, say 20 per cent, whose behaviour or progress continued to give cause for concern because it remained below that of their peers.

Hence, whatever developments take place in the education of the problematic 20 per cent, teachers will still be in a position to demand additional support in teaching them. Indeed, if they failed to demand additional guidance and support their commitment to raising standards could be called into question.

This, of course, is precisely what has happened. Ministers have seldom criticised teachers publicly for failing in their duties towards children with special needs. Nevertheless, Sir Keith Joseph, as Secretary of State, never tired of telling anyone who would listen about his concern for the educational attainments of the bottom 40 per cent. He never seemed to realise that this 40 per cent included at least 18 of the 20 per cent of the children with whom the 1981 Education Act was concerned. Critics of the educational scene from the new right argue consistently, and with some justice, that we compare well with competitor countries in the EEC in the attainments of our most able pupils, but fall down over the progress of the rest (eg. Boyson, 1988). In this conclusion there is agreement between the right and the left, though they arrive at it by totally different routes (Galloway, 1989). In other words, as O'Keefe (1987) has argued, the education system appears to be serving an academic élite of pupils. Teachers, moreover, maintain this system because they find the academic minority the easiest, most interesting and most rewarding pupils to teach.

Yet the right-wing analysis of the failures of the education system with a large minority of pupils goes further than this. In summary, it holds:

(a)   that the curriculum is excessively academic for a large proportion of pupils, failing to teach them the broadly based vocational skills they will need on leaving school;

(b)   that these curriculum failings were maintained by the former GCE/CSE examination system, on which teachers had excessive influence;

(c)   that teachers had either prevented or discouraged necessary involvement in schools by parents, local industry and the community, and were thus unresponsive to local and national needs;

(d)   that teachers, especially in inner-city areas, had used their control of the curriculum to peddle subversive left-wing ideologies;

(e) that in tackling these problems the teaching profession had shown little or no sense of urgency.

In summary, again, the government's response has been:

(a) to centralise (or nationalise?) the curriculum;

(b) to weaken the powers of the LEAs over the curriculum and over day-to-day administration of schools;

(c) to make teachers more accountable to parents and their local communities by: (i) increasing parental rights to choose their children's school; (ii) requiring schools to publish exam results; (iii) imposing conditions of service which require teachers to communicate with parents; (iv) strengthening the role of governors and increasing dramatically their responsibilities.

This overview of government thinking is not concerned with its validity nor with the possible educational and social consequences of the responses. For the present discussion, two points are important. First, there really isn't any point in trying to distinguish between Warnock's 20 per cent, Sir Keith Joseph's 40 per cent, or the even larger proportion of pupils about whom the Hargreaves Report on London secondary schools was principally concerned (ILEA, 1985). Apart from a very small minority of children with complex or severe intellectual, physical or sensory impairment they were all talking about children who were thought to present learning and adjustment difficulties. Moreover they all regarded these children's progress as a legitimate cause for public concern.

The differences between them lie in the solutions they propose. Warnock's committee and the architects of the 1981 Education Act placed their faith in the conventional special education wisdom that children must be assessed individually and a programme drawn up to meet the identified needs. On the other hand Hargreaves (1983) attacked the 'cult of individualism' that has permeated education in Britain, arguing that solutions lie in curriculum reform and organizational change. Sir Keith Joseph dithered between the two. His Lower Attaining Pupils Projects seemed to favour an alternative curriculum for less able pupils and in this sense were perhaps closer to Warnock's ideal. On the other hand, Swinnerton-Dyer (1987) has pointed out that Joseph's principal legacy on leaving the Department of Education and Science was his verdict that *all* aspects of education in Britain were in need of wide-ranging reform. This verdict provided the foundation for the 1988 Education Act with its unambiguous message that standards must be raised by curriculum reform and reorganization of schools.

The second point is that the logic of government thinking leads to the conclusion that special educational needs are a problem created *by* teachers as well as a problem *for* them. Certainly, there is provision for Statements drawn up following formal assessment under the 1981 Act to exempt children from part or all of the national curriculum requirements. Statemented children, though, will continue to form a small minority of children with special needs unless the government radically rethinks the criteria for provision of Statements. It follows that, apart from a very small minority of children, lack of motivation and underachievement must be seen as *teaching* problems. Since the problem lies with teachers, the solution must also lie with them, in the form of a more relevant curriculum taught with a greater sense of accountability to parents and governors. This is a long way from the conventional wisdom that conceptualizes special needs in terms of *learning* problems experienced by children. Here, the message is that children need special help. By implication it is they who need special attention; no responsibility rests with the curriculum, the way it is taught, or the way the school is organized.

It would be easier to applaud this belated change in the concept of special educational need if there were more evidence that the government recognized the logic of its own position. Unfortunately it seems to be in a muddle. None too subtly, teachers are held responsible for widespread pupil underachievement and lack of motivation. Yet at the same time the government almost seems to go out of its way to encourage teachers to attribute responsibility for pupils' disruptive behaviour to parents. The best example of this is the recently established Inquiry into Discipline in Schools chaired by Lord Elton. Predictably, teacher unions have seized the opportunity to assure Lord Elton's committee that: (a) the problem has got a great deal worse since the abolition of corporal punishment; (b) parents are largely to blame; (c) LEAs should never be allowed to overrule the exclusion of disruptive pupils; and (d) these pupils should be transferrred to off-site units (Sutcliffe, 1988). The rationale for the off-site units is presumably that if you put a lot of villains together this will stop them learning from each other.

The tendency to blame parents for their children's misbehaviour in school was most marked in the evidence from the National Association of Head Teachers. Even in reception classes, they claimed, conflict was 'endemic', especially in urban areas. One can, of course, criticise both the way the unions collected their 'data' and their conclusions. Their questionnaires could provide useful examples for first year undergraduate courses of all the worst faults in questionnaire design. Successive studies have shown that schools can, when they make the effort, enlist active parental support, and that this has a notably beneficial impact on children's educational progress. See, for example, J. Tizard *et al* (1982); B. Tizard *et al* (1988); Mortimore *et al* (1988). Interestingly, these studies were all carried out in inner city areas. Other evidence from Mortimore's work in the primary schools confirmed the earlier study of London secondary schools which found little consistent relationship between pupils attainments and social backgrounds on entry and their subsequent behaviour within the school (Rutter *et al,* 1979). In other words, disruptive behaviour was an infrequent problem in some schools but much more common in others, irrespective of parental background. The tendency to blame parents for children's behaviour at times when teachers are *in loco parentis* is, however, a familiar one. As Macbeth (1984) has pointed out, schools in Britain compare unfavourably with those in other EEC countries in the nature of teacher-parent liaison.

An Ideology of Control?

Politicians, like teachers, have beliefs which may or may not be based on evidence. Thus, they may believe that mixed ability classes, which by definition include pupils with special educational needs, hold back the brightest children. There is no consistent evidence for or against this view (Gregory, 1984), though it does appear that the differences within any one ability grouping system are greater than the differences between them. How politicians, or teachers, act on their beliefs depends on their values. If a school places a high value on the work of an elite group of pupils it will probably group pupils by ability. On the other hand if a high value is placed on equal opportunities for all, it may prefer mixed ability classes, and accept that this form of teaching may require teachers to learn new skills. Given effective teaching, there is no clear evidence that one system benefits any pupils' attainments more than the other.

Analysis of children's needs may appear to reflect beliefs about education and about child development, but in fact it is at least as likely to reflect political values. This is seen most clearly in discussion of children's rights. King (1981) identifies two groups which perceive children's rights, and hence their needs, in very different ways. 'Kiddy-libbers' aim to free children from the shackles of adult domination, and thus to enable them to play a fully responsible part in the running of their own lives. A.S Neill was perhaps a good example of this ideology. In contrast, are 'child-savers'. They see children:

> not as a potential challenge to the adult world, but as weak innocents in need of protection from the superior strength and experience of adults and from corruption and exploita-tion at their hands. (p.2)

An example of this ideology is the recent tendency to remove children from home on the sole basis of a highly dubious diagnosis of sexual abuse.

The point is that both kiddy-libbers and child-savers base their analysis of children's needs/rights on their own ideological values. King points out that the Declaration of the Psychological Rights of the Child (Catterall, 1980) claimed that children had the 'right to personal identity and independence and the freedom to express these'. He continues:

> Such championing of individualism would, as I understand it, run quite contrary to the political philosophy of commun-ist countries . . . So here we have what amounts to a political statement masquerading in the guise of a psychological truth. (p. 4)

Both the concept of special needs and the way a country responds to them reflect political values just as clearly. In Britain both the main political parties have expressed deep dissatisfaction with the educa-tion system in general and with its effect on academically less able pupils in particular. Very crudely, teachers have been blamed for children's low educational standards and parents for their unsatisfac-tory behaviour. Children with special needs have not featured prominently in debates about the mainstream education system leading up to the 1988 Education Act, but their progress is clearly a source of disproportionate concern to the government.

Moreover, there is a unifying theme in the government's responses to this perceived problem. Greater control is exerted over teachers *and* over children. The national curriculum and the associated attainment targets will reduce teachers' control over the curriculum. At the same time local management of schools with its consequent extended role for governors is intended to ensure much closer oversight of day-to-day running of schools than was possible in the past. The control over children themselves is exerted in a variety of ways. Attainment targets and national testing make their progress, or lack of progress, much more visible to their parents. The emphasis in most GCSE courses on regularly assessed course-work has a similar effect. For pupils who step out of line, some of them euphemistically said to have emotional and behavioural difficulties, the Secretary of State envisages removal from the mainstream into a special school or unit (Baker, 1988). Thus the trend towards increasing segregation for these pupils seems likely to continue (Advisory Centre for Education, 1980; Galloway and Goodwin, 1987), with no suggestion that they will ever be offered the somewhat dubious 'protection' of a Statement of their special needs.

Conclusion

The needs of pupils and of teachers may, as this chapter has argued, be interlinked, but whether or not this view is accepted, the concept of special educational need is influenced by political values remote from the classroom. In Britain the 1988 Education Act aims to raise standards, especially among less able pupils, by reforming the curriculum and the organization of schools. Although seldom, if ever, acknowledged by government ministers, the motivation behind the Act included dissatisfaction with the attainments and behaviour of a large majority of the pupils with whom the Warnock Report was concerned. This dissatisfaction crossed party lines. It makes little or no sense to consider policy for children with special needs in isolation from changes in the mainstream of the education system. Ultimately it is the impact of these changes that will determine the future quality of education for children with special needs.

References

ADVISORY CENTRE FOR EDUCATION (1980) *Survey on Disruptive Units,* London, ACE.
BAKER, K. (1988) 'More Replies from the Education Secretary', *British Journal of Special Education,* 5, i, pp. 6-7.
BOYSON, R. (1986) 'Follow the Lewes Priory Four', *Times Educational Supplement,* 18 March, p.4.
CATTERALL, C. (1980) 'Declaration of the Psychological Rights of the Child', *Association of Educational Psychologists Journal,* 5, iv, pp.34-7.

DEPARTMENT OF EDUCATION AND SCIENCE (1978) *Special Educational Needs* (The Warnock Report), London, DES.

GALLOWAY, D. (1989) 'Is the GERBIL a Marxist Mole?' in EVANS, P. (Ed.) *Special Education: Past, Present and Future*, Lewes, Falmer Press.

GALLOWAY, D. and GOODWIN, C. (1987) *The Education of Disturbing Children: Pupils with Learning and Adjustment Difficulties*, London, Longman.

GELSTHORPE, L. (1984) 'Diverting Children from Custody', in MULLER, D.J., BLACKMAN, D.E. and CHAPMAN, A.J. (Eds) *Psychology and the Law*, London, Wiley.

GREGORY, R.P. (1984) 'Streaming, Setting and Mixed Ability Grouping in Primary and Secondary Schools: Some Research Findings', *Educational Studies*, 10, pp. 209-26.

HARGREAVES, D.H. (1983) *The Challenge of the Comprehensive School: Culture, Curriculum, Community*, London, Routledge and Kegan Paul.

INNER LONDON EDUCATION AUTHORITY (1985) *Improving Secondary Schools*, (The Hargreaves Report), London, ILEA.

KING, M. (1981) 'Are Children's Rights Relevant?' *Association of Eductional Psychologists Journal*, 5, vi, pp. 2-7.

MACBETH, A (1984) *The Child Between: A Report on School-Family Relations in the Countries of the European Community*, EEC, (distributed by HMSO).

MORTIMORE, P., SAMMONS, P., STOLL, L., LEWIS, D. and ECOB, R. (1988) *School Matters: The Junior Years*, Wells, Open Books.

O'KEEFE, D. (1987) 'Schools as Self-Seeking Syndicates', *Economic Affairs*, April/May.

RUTTER, M., MAUGHAN, B., MORTIMORE, P. and OUSTON, J. (1979) *Fifteen Thousand Hours: Secondary Schools and their Effects on Pupils*, London, Open Books.

SIMMONS, K. (1986) 'Painful Extractions', *Times Educational Supplement*, 17 October, p. 19.

SUTCLIFFE, J. (1988) 'Suspensions Soar as Deterrent Options Dwindle', *Times Educational Supplement*, 17 June, p. A5.

SWINNERTON-DYER, P. (1987) Speech to Committee of Vice-Chancellors and Principals of UK Universities.

TIZARD, B., BLATCHFORD, P., BURKE, J., FARQUHAR, C. and PLEWIS, I. (1988) *Young Children at School in the Inner City*, Hove, Lawrence Erlbaum.

TIZARD, J., SCHOFIELD, W.M. and HEWISON, J. (1982) 'Collaboration between Teachers and Parents in Assisting Children's Reading', *British Journal of Educational Psychology*, 52, pp. 1-15.

TUTT, N. (1985) 'The Unintended Consequences of Integration, *Educational and Child Psychology*, 2, iii, pp. 30-8.

Chapter 5

Options, Choices and Special Needs in an Upper Secondary School for All: The Case of Norway

Lise Vislie

Introduction: A complex policy field

During the past two decades, the *education and training of the 16-19-year-olds* has become *a central area of policy concern in most European countries*. As far as Norway is concerned, this is largely regarded as a result of the tremendous increase in lower secondary education opportunities made possible by the introduction of the reforms in compulsory (basic) education in the 1950s and 60s, the general increase in the standard of living that took place during the same period, and a corresponding rise in educational aspirations as an effect of both these factors.

Another group of factors is related to the changes taking place in *the employment sector,* which resulted, among other things, in more demands for higher qualifications in the work force. An increase in post-compulsory education provisions has also come about as a response to a more recent need for providing alternatives to unemployment for young people.

The Norwegian Government has responded to these demands in the 70s and 80s by undertaking extensive *reforms in the upper secondary education sector,* whereby enrolments in education and training at this level have been greatly expanded, as has the variety of programmes, while at the same time the number of separate institutions normally found at this level has been reduced, a comprehensive 'integrated' school based on a full merger of the previous 'gymnasiums' and the various vocational schools and technical institutes having been established.

The scope of the problems and the complexity of the situation has led to a growing public concern and responsibility for young people, covering not only their rights to post-compulsory education, but also taking the form of a *Youth Guarantee*. The Norwegian youth guarantee entails an obligation on the part of public authorities to ensure a place in either education and training or in work for all young people up to the age of 20.

Within the wider perspective of modern *youth policies*, the focus of attention has become *all* young people in the age bracket. This is, of course, vitally important for *disadvantaged and disabled young people,* whose needs and interests, as a result, have gained more public recognition and attention in recent policies.

Finally, the fact that *matters concerning handicap and disability* have been *an area of particular policy concern* in Norway since the mid-60s should be mentioned. A White Paper to Parliament in 1966/67 stressed the importance of public responsibility and stated *normalization* as the *overall principle for policies* and further public interventions in the field. *Welfare policy principles* were strongly reflected in the White Paper and the new handicap policy grew out of, and was formulated on, this basis. The main message of the document was that instead of charity, disabled people should have *rights.* More specifically, this meant the *same rights* as other members of Norwegian society to all services and social 'goods'. The increase in public responsibility in the field should *not*, however, lead to a corresponding increase in segregated services and provisions. The aim of the reform was therefore two-fold:

a) to improve the living conditions of the disabled by increasing their command over resources which are regarded as being centrally important to general welfare (i.e. medical care, employment, education, recreation and leisure activities), and

b) to do this within the framework of those public services that are responsible for serving the general population.

Such a policy is confronted by a number of difficulties. First, if disability is defined on the basis of an existing gap between individual capabilities and the demands of the environment, disability *by definition* signalises a difficult relationship. Furthermore, disability, poor health, exclusion from the work force, low income, reduced possibilities for consumption, reduced contact and participation etc., often follow a dynamic course that is best described as a 'vicious circle'. A coherent policy on all important areas of social life and activities *may* work in the direction of breaking the 'vicious circle', but *disability* as such does not disappear. On the contrary, according to a recent Norwegian report, there is a large, and increasing, proportion of disability in Norway (Barth, 1987).

Looking at disability from a welfare perspective, the emphasis is on living conditions and the fact that disabled persons normally face *restricted possibilities for choice*. In improving the living conditions of disabled people, by providing opportunities for them, the welfare state faces another dilemma: that of increasing the dependency of disabled people by making them *more* dependent on the decisions and measures of others. According to Barth:

> Disabled persons are more dependent on the decisions and measures of others. Members of one's own household and political authorities have a greater and more direct impact on the life of a disabled person than of others. This is an important dimension of a disabled person's welfare, and must be taken more strongly into account in the future. The individual should have greater freedom of choice . . . (p.123).

Other reports which have recently appeared in the field have stressed the same points (see, for example, OECD, 1988; Oliver, 1988). However, the emphasis on choice, client control and decision-making is not only linked to the disability and social policy fields, but is found in most other policy areas and related documents as well. In youth policies, for instance, the Norwegian state guarantees either employment or education for young people up to the age of 20, preferably 'according to their own choice'. The reform in upper secondary education rests on the principle that students shall have 'the greatest freedom of choice' possible among different areas of study and courses.

However, the reality is different. Given the present trends in the employment sector, opportunities for young people are steadily shrinking, and thus the 'Youth Guarantee' offers mostly educational provisions. Under such circumstances upper secondary education is gradually becoming 'obligatory'. And as will be shown in more detail below, a number of restrictions or 'barriers' to 'free choice' are built into upper secondary provisions as well.

Freedom of choice is an ideal which rarely exists in modern societies. *Dependency* is much more prevalent. As Oliver stresses:

> An inevitable consequence of living in industrial society is that we live in a condition of mutual dependency (p. 22) and
> . . . welfare states have created whole groups of classes or people who become dependent upon the state for education, health care, financial support and indeed, any other provision the state is prepared to offer (p. 2).

> The dependence of disabled people therefore, is not a feature
> which marks them out as different in kind from the rest of the
> population but different in degree (p. 1).

This chapter will not discuss the welfare state in general, nor the
more special dependency problems related to an expanding welfare
state (the public sector is still increasing in Norway). The main
purpose of this chapter is to review current policies and practices in
Norway concerning *the provision of education and training options* that
follow compulsory schooling — particularly from the *perspective of young
people with disabilities*. The *existing options* offered at this level will be
looked at, and an attempt will be made to describe to what extent, or
how, they can be seen as *representing options* for further education and
training for *young disabled people*. The *choices* made by young people
will be analyzed according to various sets of national data, i.e. mainly
from *the way the system of options is presently organized and filled* by
young people, including young disabled persons.

Thus the approach is to start by first asking what the options and
the present scope of 'freedom of choice' in education are at this level
in general, and, secondly, by asking about openings for special
populations. Briefly, the argument for this approach is that if the
problems are not seen — and subsequently attacked — in context,
the impact of policy will easily become an uncontrolled and
ever-increasing dependency in society in general, and an even
greater degree of dependency among disabled populations. Thus the
chapter has been *inspired* by the views presented above concerning
the policy dilemmas of the welfare state and the increasing
dependency problems in modern societies.

Before turning to the data and the analyses, a brief note is
included on the problems connected with doing national reviews on
educational policies and implementation in Norway. Over the past
decades, a process of decentralization has been undertaken by the
Authorities and, as a result, local and regional authorities as well as
local schools at all levels have to a very large extent been released
from detailed central control (local politicians, administrators and
teachers have been made fully responsible for their own political and
professional affairs). For most purposes this can be regarded as a very
positive development. One of the problems is that information
about how the system as a whole is working is largely lacking. The
Ministry is putting a lot of resources (of all kinds) into the system,
but does very little in terms of evaluating or monitoring it. The
situation was commented on critically by the OECD examiners in

their report on educational policy in Norway (OECD, 1988). As a consequence, the Ministry is now planning to establish a better database.

In addition to these general Norwegian problems, it will, and in fact should always be *difficult* to describe an integrated system in terms of precise information (statistical figures) concerning the extent and impact of special populations, programmes or arrangements within the system. In analyzing an integrated system, information concerning *who* or *what* is *not* included in the figures is frequently more informative than the positive facts given, and thus it is also interesting to study the statistical 'gaps'.

Education in Norway — policy principles and strategies

A fundamental *aim of the educational policy* in Norway during this century has been to raise the general educational level of the population *as a whole,* and to provide *equal educational opportunities for all.* Historically, the Norwegian approach to this objective has been closely linked with *the comprehensive, common school model.* In 1920 a common school system was established in Norway for the whole seven year period of compulsory education. The system developed in Norway has been characterized by neighbourhood organization, a common curriculum, no streaming of pupils according to ability, and, in principle, automatic promotion of pupils from lower to higher grades. After the end of World War II, compulsory schooling extended to cover nine years, a reform which was fully implemented in accordance with the above mentioned principles with the passing of the Education Act in 1969.

When the new overall policy orientation related to handicap and disability was introduced in the mid 60s, it had an immediate effect on educational policies. A long planned and extensive expansion of provision within the special (segregated) school system was stopped by Parliament. As an alternative the Education Committee formulated a policy programme for the *integration of disabled pupils* in education, which was presented to Parliament in 1968. As soon as the nine years compulsory education reform was fully implemented throughout the country by the passing of the Education Act 1969, a Royal commission was to prepare for a full merger of this legislation and the Special School Act 1951. Amendments to the Compulsory Education Act were finally passed by Parliament in 1975.

In the meantime a new Upper Secondary Education Act —

based on the same principles — had already been passed by Parliament the year before (1974). Both reforms came into force on 1 January 1976.

As a result of this legislation all rights to education for disabled persons were regulated according to the principle of *normalization*. All separate legislation was abolished and *equal rights to (compulsory and) upper secondary education for all young persons,* including those with special education needs, were formally established.

At the same time *the right to education* was also *reformulated.* According to present Norwegian policy and legislation all children and young persons have *the right to an education in accordance with their own needs, interests, and capabilities.* Since 1976 — when both acts came into force — this principle refers to compulsory *and* upper secondary education. There is no lower limit to this principle and thus handicapped pupils are also included.

Historically, there has also been *a change in policy strategies* over the century, which is also worth noting. Up to the end of World War II, the basic idea behind the comprehensive, common school model was that 'all are equal, and shall be treated equally — no one shall be favoured'. Over the years it has been realized that *the problems of inequality* are complex and intricate and cannot successfully be dealt with as easily as that. The principle of the common school is still strong in Norwegian education, but to this principle has been added a *principle of positive discrimination.* The basic insight behind this change is that *a school for all* has to *accept inequality,* and must *actively assist* children and young persons who, because of social background or environment, sex, ethnicity, mental or physical handicap, have a special difficulty in becoming integrated in school and society and sharing its opportunities on equal terms.

Positive discrimination is achieved through various measures, of which *funding policies* are generally considered the most important by ensuring that more resources are allocated to the economically weaker areas, to disadvantaged populations or to special programmes. There is also a series of other measures, more related to the *style of provision* (encouraging greater participation in education by under-represented or special groups, for example), and adhering fairly strictly to supplementing regular education and curricula rather than providing alternative educational experiences such as special classes or schools (OECD, 1983).

At present, special education and integration at the post-compulsory level is a priority area within educational policy in Norway. Partly this is a result of *at least* one generation of handicapped children and their families having had fairly good opportunities for obtaining integrated education at the compulsory school level. An overall impression of policy implementation and present practice has been documented elsewhere (Dahl *et al.*, 1982) and shows that in 1981 less than 1 per cent of the total pupil population (7-15 year olds) was educated *outside* the ordinary schools and classes (i.e. in special schools or classes or in social or medical institutions). A follow-up control on data for the school year 1984/85 showed that this percentage was then down to 0.66 per cent of the total pupil population.

According to national estimates approximately 12 per cent of the pupil population receive some kind of special education, mostly on a permanent basis, but with a varying number of hours of special teaching per week during the school year. In statistical terms compulsory education covers 100 per cent of young population in the respective age groups. According to other (more qualitative) information we have reason to believe that there are actually very few 'drop-outs' from this system, and the 'drop-out'-problem (at the youth stage of compulsory schooling) is also considered relatively small (Dahl, *et al.*, 1982).

It is this *policy of integration at the compulsory school level* which is now being extended to the next level. Basically, the strategies and policy measures are more or less the same as those which have — to some extent successfully — been applied over a decade or two to obtain integrated provision for handicapped pupils in compulsory education.

Leaving compulsory education — options and choices at the post-compulsory level

The importance of choice, search and experimentation during adolescence is generally stressed in modern societies. Consequently, recent reforms and policy intervention of various kinds have in many ways extended the basis for choice at the post-compulsory level, at the same time as the majority of the young population — including groups for whom such opportunities were out of the question only a few decades ago — have been given access to further education and training.

But there are less favourable sides to this development as well. *The decision process has become much more difficult,* partly because the prospects for the future are generally uncertain, but also because the employment value of many programmes is difficult to foresee. *A range of restrictions* are also built into the system, and the system has become more difficult to investigate and understand in terms of variation and consequences. Thus *choice is easily getting mixed up with allocation and selection* (OECD, October 1984).

The aim of the outline in the present section is to illustrate some of the present complexities in the field as related to the Norwegian context and to draw attention to the 'trivial' fact that for *young people with disabilities* the transition process is probably characterized by *less choice* and *more allocation*.

As a first approach to this outline some data on *compulsory school leavers* will be given. After nine years of compulsory schooling, young Norwegians are, in principle, free to choose whether they wish to continue schooling at the post-compulsory level or to do something else. According to national figures, the large majority of pupils finishing compulsory education in the spring are in some kind of education by the following autumn. This trend has been increasing over the last decade (for example, the percentage was 80.7 in 1978 and 87.6 in 1984. No data is available for special populations).

These figures illustrate the present trends in young peoples' choices in general terms, but not the individual dilemmas or the controversial issues involved. The fact that *about 94 per cent* of school leavers in 1983 *applied* for a place in post-compulsory education, and that by October the same year, *only about 87% were in education* (all types) is one indication of the present problems. We don't know how many would have preferred to have some kind of work if the possibilities in the employment sector had been better for young people, and to what extent this is a problem for individuals. We can only register that only 6 per cent of the cohort *does not apply for further education and training* upon leaving compulsory education (less than 5 per cent in 1988).

Another problem is that many who are, in principle, accepted, are not admitted to the type of school or area of study of their first preference (in some cases not even their second or third preference). A recent OECD report (October 1984) on policies for post-compulsory education and training stresses the point that for more and more young people *the problem is no longer that of finding a place at the post-compulsory education level, but that of entering the areas of study or types of programmes of their choice.*

Turning to the Norwegian situation *the various options available* to pupils when leaving compulsory schooling and the relative import-ance attached to different provisions in terms of student enrolment are roughly indicated by the data given in Table 1.

Table 1: Percentage of pupils finishing compulsory education 1982, 1983 and 1984 by type of school at 1st October the following year

	10th grade provision	Upper secondary school	Folk high school	Other post-compulsory schools	Not in education
1982	4.3	75.0	3.3	1.1	16.3
1983	5.2	79.9	3.3	1.2	12.5
1984	5.4	78.3	2.9	1.0	12.4

Sources: The Central Bureau of Statistics – Educational statistics for Primary and Lower Secondary Schools in 1985, 1986 and 1987.

As mentioned above and as shown by the data presented in Table 1 *the main option* for young people leaving compulsory education is *more* education — note that only about 12 per cent of the cohorts of 1983 and 1984 was not in education the following autumn. Note also that *the main options within education* for compulsory school leavers are presently found within the upper secondary school (close to 80 per cent). Less than 10 per cent continue their education in provisions *not* covered by the main structure.

The *10th grade provisions* (organized on a voluntary basis by the communes and attached to the youth stage of the compulsory schools) and *the folk high schools* (run partly by voluntary organizations, partly by the county school authorities) enrolled only small proportions of the cohorts, while a small number of 'other schools' as a total attracted even fewer students.

The latter category includes the *State Special Schools* which are of particular interest here. These schools may be regarded as a reminiscence of the Special School Act, which was abolished when the new Education Acts came into force in 1976. The State still *runs* eleven institutions classified as upper secondary special schools for designated categories of handicapped (all residential), but the respective county authority will have to *pay* for any student from their catchment area who is placed there. The number of students enrolled in these schools has been relatively stable and small over the past few years (435 students in 1985, with the schools not filled to capacity).

While the State Special Schools only provide options for

disabled young people, mainly for pupils who have been in similar school provisions at the compulsory level, all the other schools referred to in Table 1 represent *options for all*. As a result of the Upper Secondary Education Act, 1974 and the yearly expansion in provisions under this Act, the relative importance of this new structure — for young disabled people as well — has steadily increased, and pupils' choices have also moved in this direction. For example, even the 10th grade provisions, which tended to increase a little in the 80s, are as popular as they were. In fact few actually have the 10th grade courses as their (first) choice at the end of compulsory education. The provision normally absorbs many of the students not admitted to upper secondary schools, some of the early drop-outs from the same schools, and some who try but do not succeed in finding work at the end of compulsory education. There is little doubt that a number of young people with *mild to moderate disabilities* (learning disabled) belong to this group.

The folk high schools have a long tradition in Norwegian education. They have no specific vocational purpose, but offer a variety of courses, mostly of a general orientation, emphasizing certain subjects/fields such as aesthetics, sports, environmental protection, media, etc. Many of these schools offer programmes for disabled young people, also severely multi-handicapped persons, *as part of their ordinary provision*. While attending a course all students are accommodated in student hostels, which may make the provision partricularly attractive for many handicapped. In spite of this the folk high schools are presently not filled to capacity.

It should be noted that there are considerable regional varia-tions in terms of these figures, which may be seen as another example of the complex relationship between public supply of provisions and student choices at this level.

Alternatives, choices and special needs in schools under the Upper Secondary Education Act 1974

Post-compulsory education at the intermediate level was restructured and organized within a common framework in the 70s (the new Act came in force in 1976). In the new upper secondary school, general, technical and vocational education are integrated into *one system* under *the governance of the county authorities*. The purpose of the integration strategy was to give equal and full upper secondary status to all education and training options at this level. All students take a common set of core subjects, in addition to the special or optional subjects which indicate their particular study orientation.

Normally the upper secondary school offers three years of education (basic courses and advanced courses at two levels). Students may, however, finish school after either one, two or three years, since each school year constitutes, as far as possible, a complete unit in terms of courses.

According to the present structure the students basically have to choose between *three main tracks* of upper secondary education: the general area of study, the vocational area of study, the 2-year basic courses.

An *area of study* roughly corresponds to the same type of education previously provided by independent schools. Nine different areas of study are now included within the same organizational structure. Each school may offer one or more areas of study. Some schools ('integrated schools') administer up to six or seven areas of study.

Approximately 70 per cent of all 16-19 year olds are presently enrolled in upper secondary education in Norway, compared to 82 per cent in West Germany, 71 per cent in USA and 38 per cent in UK (OECD, 1984). Data now indicate that 2-3 years of post-compulsory education or training is gradually becoming the norm in this country. The present *total capacity* of the upper secondary school roughly corresponds to *more* than three cohorts (age groups 16-19). About 20 per cent of all students enrolled are *older* than this (demands for upper secondary education have increased in later years, particularly among those aged between 20-24).

Concerning *provisions for disabled young people* several sections of the Upper Secondary Education Act 1974 are of particular interest, of which the following should be emphasized:

— handicapped students are entitled to more than three years of education
— special education shall be provided to students who, according to expert opinion, need such provisions
— handicapped students are entitled to school transport (and other facilities)
— students shall have access to pedagogical-psychological services
— the county school authorities are instructed to consider and include the needs of disabled young persons (within the catchment area) in all planning activities.

In the remaining part of this section the question of options presently available for disabled persons within the new structure will be considered by looking at: (a) admission regulations, (b) the expansion and present volume of special education, and (c) organizational aspects and content profiles of special education programmes.

Admission regulations

According to the Act *entrance* to upper secondary education was not restricted by any minimum requirements, and the law provided legal openings for students from special schools or programmes to enter the schools. However, as the new schools had capacity problems, particularly in the first years, admission had to be regulated.

Admission regulations (established by the Ministry) were generally based on a series of different criteria (marks, age, previous applications, work experience, etc.). As a particular measure the Ministry also introduced *a quota arrangement,* whereby the county authorities were first instructed to *reserve 2%* of all available student places within the region for students with *special education needs,* or for students who for *social or medical reasons* (according to expert opinion) could claim admittance to a particular type of study. This means that two admission systems have been operated by the county authorities, *the joint admission system* (mechanically operated) and *the individualized quota/special system.*

In 1981 a first proposal of giving handicapped students *admission by priority* was put before Parliament. The proposal raised much discussion. Nevertheless, in 1982 admission by priority for the group in question was stipulated by law, but, for the time being, not made effective. Meanwhile it was decided to intensify the educational innovation programmes in the field, to gradually increase the number of students admitted according to the quota arrangements, and to increase the transfer of funds to the counties correspondingly.

From then onwards the number of students admitted according to quota arrangements rapidly increased (in fact in many counties beyond the minimums specified by Parliament). In 1985 the national average had reached *5 per cent.* It was then decided to give up the quota arrangements and to transfer to the priority principle. The new principle took effect from 1 January 1987.

The priority principle has only been effective a short time and national figures concerning applicants and students admitted are not yet available (that the number admitted makes up more than 5 per cent of the total intake is, of course, beyond doubt). The law stipulates admission by priority to upper secondary education for applicants aged 16-20 who, according to expert opinion, need 'tilrettelagt opplæring' (English translation difficult: 'adjusted' or (specially) 'prepared' or 'arranged' training. 'Special education' will be used when referring to this provision in the following.) Notice particularly that the right is not linked to any categories of handicap, but primarily to *needs* as understood and presented by the applicants themselves. *Decisions* are made by a small commission (in principle a democratic political body) appointed by the county school author-ities, who also hear the opinions of the experts. Therefore the role of the expert is, in principle, that of giving advice, not of making decisions. The impact of the professionals, whether they are teachers, educational psychologists or medical doctors, is, of course, still substantial.

The regulations are still a matter of some discussion. It is, for example, argued that the criteria for giving priority are not precise enough and are therefore not consistently practiced from one county to another. The role of the experts is another issue. Two areas of 'expert opinion' are distinguished: one concerns the individual applicants and individual conditions, the other concerns the possibi-lities inherent in the school system (for differentiation, innovation and the provision of alternatives). How, and by whom, is the latter area of expertise, which may be considered even more important than the former, to be more effectively included in the process (Aarnes, 1987)?

The expansion and present volume of special education

Data presented above concerning the admission registrations can also be used as rough estimates on *the volume of special education at this stage.* However, there is not full correspondence here. For example, *not all* students admitted on special terms over the years have actually needed or in fact obtained extra support or special education in upper secondary education. According to information reported by the counties in 1982, when the total quota arrangements made up 4.1 per cent of the total intake, only 1.8 per cent of all students were reported to be obtaining extra support. In 1983 the corresponding figures were 4.3 per cent and 2.9 per cent.

According to the data presented in Table 2 the total number of students registered as obtaining special education in upper secondary schools (organized by the county authorities) was 1,020 in 1976. The year after, the numbers had more than doubled, and in 1982, 4,648 students were registered in such provisions. More information concerning the present volume of special education is presented in Table 3.

Table 2: Students obtaining special education in upper secondary schools by types of organization 1976-1982

School year	Total no. of students	No. of students in special classes/groups			Extra support to students in regular classes (N)	
1976	1020	874	86%		146	14%
1977	2380	881	79%	approx.	500	21%
1978	4330	1479	35%		2815	65%
1979	4806	1573	33%		3233	67%
1980	4400	1743	40%		3233	60%
1981	4412	1848	42%		2564	58%
1982	4648	2047	45%		2551	55%

Sources: Ministry of Education annual budget reports to Parliament. The figures cover only provisions organized by the counties (the State Upper Secondary School provisions are not included).

Organisational aspects

The following arrangements are operated by the county authorities:
External organization The county may 'buy' educational service (a place) in a State Special School, a social or medical institution etc.;
Special classes/groups (maximum four or eight students per group depending on the area of study) established on a permanent basis at a local school;
Special groups combined with education in ordinary classes for individual students for part of the programme;
Full integration/special education in regular classes;
Training in work.

Data for each type of arrangement is not easily available. In Table 2 (NB information is *not* given for *all* students admitted under the quota arrangements for the respective years, see above) provisions are classified in two different categories — the special classes/groups (all types) and individual support to students in regular classes. According to the data presented, the proportion of

Table 3: Students in special education programmes by area of study.
(Registrations made 1 October 1984 and 1985)

Areas of study	Total no. of students in special education courses	
	1984/85	1985/86
General area of study	550	819
Vocational areas of study		
Fishing trade	–	4
Commercial and clerical	320	289
Technical and industrial	1920	2017
Aesthetic subjects	150	146
Physical education/sports	–	–
Domestic science	590	602
Agricultural subjects	50	49
Maritime subjects	–	3
Social services and health subjects	–	11
Unknown area of study	1110	1082
Total	4690	5022

Source: The table is constructed on the basis of data reported by the Council for Upper Secondary Education and registrations made by the local schools.

students obtaining special support in special classes decreased rapidly from 1976 (when it made up 86 per cent of the provision) to 1979 (when only 33 per cent were in special groups). In 1982 45 per cent of the students were in special groups, while 55 per cent obtained extra support as students of regular classes. Comparable data for subsequent years are not available, but there is no indication that the distribution has changed much over the past years. Thus it can be concluded that a little less than half of all students receiving special education are provided for in special groups, while the majority are provided for in integrated settings.

Organizational arrangements differ across study areas: the smaller special classes or groups (maximum four students) are linked to the vocational areas of study; the other groups (maximum eight students) to the general areas of study (maximum regular class norms are fifteen and thirty respectively). There are more groups of four in operation than groups of eight, and in terms of absolute numbers the groups of four also enrol more students. This is mainly an effect of more special education students being admitted to the vocational areas of study (see below), but probably also an effect of this being the type of special education which has hitherto been the most profitable arrangement for the counties vis-a-vis the government (until 1986, when the financial transfer from central to regional/local governments system was changed to a block grant system).

In many cases the special education provisions are *formally* registered as special groups of four or eight by the county authorities, while the local school may in fact operate the provision more in accordance with a full integration model or at least partly as a special group/education in regular classes provision and if the schoolteachers so wish. Generally, decision-making concerning the actual organization of special programmes is left to the school (for more information, see Vislie, 1985).

As special classes are mostly organized on a permanent basis, the students in such arrangements will normally receive a full time special education programme. The 'extra-support' category covers a mixture of flexible arrangements and the extent of support provided to individual students will also vary (the number of hours per week allowed for special support normally being specified for each individual at the time of admission).

Content profiles of special education programmes

Finally, some information concerning *the content of special education.* First of all, a distinction must be made between all kinds of extra support in regular subjects, mostly provided to students registered as regular class/course students and obtaining special support on that basis, and the programmes organised and *designated* as special education programmes. Only the content profiles of the latter type of programmes will be considered here.

Generally speaking, special education programmes may be said to cover a *wide variety of educational activities,* from introductory programmes for students with a foreign mother tongue, to what can be considered mainly as extended compulsory education programmes for 16-19-year-olds, ADL-training programmes, a variety of so called 'preparatory' programmes, and other courses more closely linked to the regular areas of study, but with a modified course content or a slower pace.

Table 3 classifies all students enrolled in programmes identified by the schools as full-time 'special education courses' in the years 1984/85 and 1985/86 by area of study.

Again, it is emphasized that these figures do not cover all students admitted to the school on special terms, nor all students receiving some kind of special education in the respective school years. For example, the number of students covered by the information given in Table 3 for 1985/86 makes up only 2.5 per cent of the total number of students in upper secondary education, while the corresponding national figure for students admitted under special terms was 5 per cent at that time.

According to the information provided in Table 3, the majority of special education programmes are formally linked to vocational areas of study, particularly in the technical and industrial area. In view of the large number of total student enrolments in the general area of study, the number of special education programmes offered within this area, and the number of students in such programmes, is generally very low. Whether special education programmes *should be* vocational or general in orientation is a principle point of discussion among the programme planners and other experts. Many argue in favour of vocational programmes 'to ensure that disabled students get jobs'. Others emphasize the importance of prolonged training in basic skills and general orientation.

Only one of the identified special education programmes was *an advanced course.* The vast majority of the special programmes therefore only provide basic courses at a very limited level (compare here in particular the high number of students enrolled in courses of 'unknown' area of study in Table 3). There is reason to believe that most students who enrol in the special programmes spend up to two to three (sometimes four) years in upper secondary education, but mostly by adding basic courses (following a 'horizontal' instead of a 'vertical' line of progress). This may be the fate of other special education/support students as well, particularly if they are enrolled in vocational areas of study. Here a wide range of the advanced courses have insufficient capacity, and many students who have completed a (regular) basic course will find it difficult to get into the advanced courses to obtain a full vocational training.

In terms of content the types of special education programmes may vary a lot from region to region. To some extent the course content offered seems to represent geographical characteristics as well as regional differences in employment/economic conditions (another indication of 'market/job-oriented' programme planning).

Options open to post-compulsory education for young people living in institutions

Many young people live permanently, or stay for shorter or longer periods of their life, in *social or medical institutions*. Educational options for these typical client groups are important and should therefore not be overlooked in this review.

The category covers different types of institutions, e.g. hospitals, special institutions for (severely) mentally retarded or for people with emotional/behavioural disorders. In many of these institutions schools are established, but while in general compulsory education is fairly well provided for the 7-16-year-olds living in such institutions, *post-compulsory provisions are still insufficient* (for example, many do not obtain any such provision at all, provision is limited, there are few alternatives, etc.).

Under the present circumstances, the main question is whether these young people obtain any post-compulsory provision at all. According to data provided by a national survey undertaken in 1981/82 (by the Council for Upper Secondary Education) the total number of clients in social and medical institutions *aged 16-19* was *1,044,* of which *72 per cent obtained some kind of educational provision.* The largest group was the mentally retarded (737), of which only 15 per cent did not obtain any educational provision. These figures can be compared with the overall national figures, according to which about 70 per cent of all 16-19-year-olds are presently in some kind of upper secondary education.

Conclusion

Overall trends in the recent quantitative development of upper secondary education provisions for students with special education needs have been examined above. This chapter concentrates on significant aspects of these trends, such as the *number of students admitted* to upper secondary education on *special terms* (quota/priority arrangements), *the volume of special education,* different *organizational forms* and the *content profiles* of special programmes.

From the above figures it is evident that as part of the general expansion in upper secondary provisions in Norway over the last decade, an increasing number of disabled students or students with special education needs have also been admitted to secondary schools. Two to three years of upper secondary education has become a general norm, and there are indications that this norm also applies to disabled student populations. The educational rights of disabled students have been ensured by applying quota/priority regulations and procedures at the entrance level.

The figures also indicate the prevailing modes of attending to special education needs in Norway, in particular the different forms of organizing special education provisions and the content profiles of special programmes developed to meet 'special needs'. According to the overall (national) figures presented, special education in upper secondary education in Norway is presently provided as *a mixture of integrated and segregated* organization and programming. The vast majority of provisions is, however, organized and linked to regular upper secondary schools. For this and other reasons, it is believed that there is more flexibility of arrangements in practice than that which is indicated by the figures. Certainly there are substantial differences in policies and practice among counties, and even among local schools within the same county, which emerge if figures for the counties are considered separately, or if information based on more qualitative data (case studies) are inspected.

References

AARNES, A. (1987) 'Inntak i videregående skole. De sakkyndiges rolle ved behandling av søknader fra funksjonshemmede om fortrinnsrett.' Notat. RVO's konferanse om tilrettelagt opplæring i Trondheim.

BARTH, E. (1987) 'Funksjonshemmede i Norge. En analyse av antall, helse og levekår på grunnlag av Helseundersøkelsen 1985', *Gruppe for helsetjenesteforskning*, Rapport nr. 6.

DAHL, M., TANGERUD, H. and VISLIE, L. (1982) *Integration of Handicapped Pupils in Compulsory Education in Norway*, Oslo, Universitetsforlaget.

OECD (1983) *The Education of Minority Groups: An enquiry into problems and practices of fifteen countries*, Aldershot, Gower.

OECD (January 1988) *Disability and Adult Status: Concepts, Policy Issues and Practical Dilemmas*, Educational Monographs, no. 4.

OECD (February 1988) 'Reviews of National Policies for Education, Norway' Draft.

OLIVER, M. (1988) 'Social Policy and Disability: The Creation of Dependency'. Paper presented at Symposium on Adult Status for Youth with Disabilities, Sigtuna (Sweden) 13-15 April.

VISLIE, L. (1985) 'Integration of Handicapped Students in Upper Secondary Education: A Case Study of a Norwegian School', in OECD, *Integration of the Handicapped in Secondary Schools: Five Case Studies*, Paris, OECD/CERI.

Chapter 6

The Nigerian National Policy on Special Education: A Reality or a Myth?

Theresa B. Abang

Introduction

The question of policy and practice has for too long been a subject of great concern to many concerned individuals and organizations in most countries. Discrepancies that exist between policies and practice are not peculiar to developing countries *per se*. No doubt in every human endeavour, there is always the ideal and the practice, what is and what ought to be. This fact cuts across all spheres of life, affecting policies governing nations and their implementation, and the Nigerian Policy on Special Education has not escaped it. There is no doubt that a disjunction between rhetoric and practice exists, as may be the case in many other developing nations. Policies ought to effect the desired changes, but this is not always the case. Although my discussion will be focused principally on the Nigerian Policy on Special Education, I am certain that the Nigerian situation is not too different from that of other developing nations.

This chapter will seek, therefore, to examine the Nigerian National Policy on Special Education in all its ramifications, to see how it is being implemented and where it has failed. We will examine the factors militating against its successful implementation and how these difficulties could be remedied for the good of Special Education in Nigeria. The identification of Nigeria's problems and their solutions would no doubt profit most other developing nations as well.

A Chinese sage said, 'A journey of a thousand miles begins with the first step'. In this context, we have many thousands of steps to take in bringing adequate services to many unreached disabled people in Nigeria and other developing countries. This can only be achieved through well thought out policies which can be implemented.

The Policy on Special Education

In 1977, when the Nigerian National Policy on Special Education was introduced, it was seen as a hopeful sign for the future for the child with special educational needs. Among other things, the policy provides education for all handicapped and gifted children and aims to give concrete meaning to the idea of equalizing educational opportunities for all children; to provide adequate education for all handicapped children and adults; and to provide opportunities for exceptionally gifted children to develop at their own pace. Although this policy has some flaws, nevertheless there has to be a beginning if a change is to be effected. For the purpose of giving others the opportunity to examine the Nigerian Policy on Special Education critically and make useful suggestions, I will quote the entire policy here.

The Policy has only four paragraphs with Subsections. It is as follows:

(53) Special Education is the Education of Children and Adults who have learning difficulty because of different sorts of handicap such as blindness, partial sightedness, deafness, hardness of hearing, mental retardation, social maladjustment, physical handicap, etc., due to circumstances of birth, inheritance, social position, mental and physical health patterns or accident in later life. As a result, a few children and adults are unable to cope with the normal school organization and methods.

(54) There are also the special gifted children who are intellectually precocious and find themselves insufficiently challenged by the programme of the normal school and who may take to stubbornness and apathy in resistance to it. Government has already directed that all children, including the gifted as well as those with physical, mental and learning difficulties, must be provided for under the educational system. The corollary of Universal Primary Education (UPE) therefore is that special education arrangements must be made for the handicapped and exceptionally gifted.

(55) The purpose and objectives of Special Education should be:

(a) to give concrete meaning to the idea of equalizing educational opportunities for all children, their physical, mental, emotional disabilities not withstanding;

(b) to provide adequate education for all handicapped children and adults in order that they may fully play their roles in the development of the Nation;

(c) to provide opportunities for exceptionally gifted children to develop at their own pace in the interest of the Nation's economic and technological development.

(56) (1) The Federal Ministry of Education will set up a Committee to coordinate special educational activities in collaboration with the Ministries of Health, Social Welfare and Labour.

(2) A census will be taken of all handicapped children and adults by age, sex and type; and schools will be obligated to make yearly returns of children who could be classified as so highly gifted as to attract national attention as to their potential and the granting of scholarship to them;

(3) Considering the importance of highly trained and efficient personnel in the area of Special Education, Government accepts the responsibility for making provision for training teachers in Special Education as well as the supportive staff required by the schools, colleges, clinics and centres in this area.

(4) As soon as is feasible, all Teacher Training Colleges will provide general and basic education to all prospective teachers who would teach in normal schools but who require such knowledge to identify and help handicapped children. In addition, the Ministries of Education will arrange crash courses of in-service training for all teachers of handicapped children.

(5) Government has decided that integration is the most realistic form of Special Education since handicapped children are eventually expected to live in the society. Therefore, it has already accepted that special classes and units will be provided in ordinary schools under the Universal Primary Education Scheme. These will be well staffed and equipped. However, special schools where necessary will be established for the handicapped, mentally retarded and other disabled children.

(6) The Ministries of Education will in consultation with the appropriate bodies provide special programmes for gifted children but within the normal educational set-up.

(7) The education of handicapped and gifted children will be free at all levels up to the University level where possible.

(8)   Vocational schools will be made to reserve places for further education of handicapped children and adults. Other multi-purpose vocational schools will be established as needs arise. Government will provide suitable employment opportunities for handicapped workers, and the Ministry of Social Development, Youth and Sports will be requested to examine the possibilities of establishing sheltered workshops for those handicapped, who after training cannot bid on equal terms with others for recruitment into Commerce and Industries. The Committee on Special Education and the National Council for the Rehabilitation of the Disabled will be fully involved in these plans.

(9)   Children's clinics will be attached to most hospitals, for early identification of handicapped children and for curative measures and medical care before and after they reach the age for primary schooling.

(10)   Ministries of Health, Education and Social Welfare, Social Development and Labour will work jointly on most programmes for handicapped children and the National Council on Special Education will be composed to reflect this collective responsibility.

As observed in the Policy, the Nigerian Policy on Special Eduction advocates education for all handicapped and gifted children in Nigeria. As Section (54) clearly states:

Government has already directed that all children including the gifted as well as those with physical, mental and learning difficulties must be provided for under the educational system.

The question arises — what are the realities now?

Reality of the Situation

There is one phenomenon common among developing countries, which is the fact that heroic ideas are generally conceived and put on paper but rarely implemented.

In the Nigerian situation, eleven years have passed and an examination of this policy and its implementation will no doubt expose this fact and suggest a course of action. For educators in Nigeria, the Nigerian Policy on Education, of which Special

Education is a part, is a very important document which is meant to guide us in the practice of an effective education. The document is short, but comprehensive, and contains in it principles, plans and in some cases, a course of action which is aimed at strengthening educational practices in Nigeria. This no doubt goes to show the importance placed on education by the Nigerian Government, including Special Education. Nigeria no doubt realizes that education is an investment both in human and material resources of any nation. On this Briggs writes:

> Education is a long term investment by the State to make itself a better place in which to live and a better place in which to make a living.

As stated earlier, I found the policy on Special Education wanting in some aspects. For example, the Policy defines Special Education as:

> the education of children and adults who have learning difficulties because of different sorts of handicaps; blindness, partial sightedness, deafness, physical handicaps, etc. due to circumstances of birth, inheritance, social position, mental and physical health patterns or accident in later life. As a result a few children and adults are unable to cope with the normal school organization and methods. (Section (53))

This definition is somewhat inadequate in that it only emphasizes those for whom Special Education is meant but not what Special Education really is. This is a clear case of misplaced emphasis. Samuel Kirk (1979) offers a good definition of Special Education when he says that it refers to those aspects of education which are applied to handicapped and gifted children but not usually used with the majority of average children. Special education can further be said to be an adaptation or modification of, or an addition to, school practices intended for normal children. Special education therefore is not altogether a new invention. One is only adding something to what already exists to enable the 'special child' to learn.

The objectives as contained in the Policy are as follows:

> (a) to give concrete meaning to the idea of equalizing educational opportunities for all children, their physical, mental, emotional disabilities notwithstanding;
> (b) to provide adequate education for all handicapped children and adults in order that they may fully play their roles in the development of the Nation;

(c) to provide opportunities for exceptionally gifted children to develop at their own pace in the interest of the Nation's economic and technological development.

These objectives no doubt are indisputably good. One may like to examine what is obtainable in practice. Are these objectives being realized? The first objective states that, ideally, equal opportunity would be given to all children, their disabilities notwithstanding.

For the purpose of this chapter, I will first examine whether disabled people have been given equal opportunities with their normal counterparts, as stated in the Policy. This point needs to be discussed with regard to admissions into institutions of higher learning. Here, disabled students are given the opportunity to sit for National Entrance Examinations. These include the Common Entrance Examination for admission into secondary schools, the West African Examination Certificate at the end of the secondary school and the Joint Academic Matriculation Examination (JAME) which qualifies one for admission into the University. All disabled students are entitled to take these examinations. For blind people, provision to transcribe the question papers into braille is generally made prior to the examination date. The problem of unequal opportunity arises after such students have passed the entrance examination and are being considered for admission.

Some institutions discriminate in admitting disabled students on the grounds that they lack adequate facilities and personnel. Even when given admission, some students encounter untold difficulty in an environment not designed with them in mind. In the case of people who are physically disabled, movement is a problem. There may not be curbs from the parking place to the buildings neither are ramps provided in place of steps. This poses problems for those in wheelchairs. If there is to be equal opportunity, pavements and ramps must be provided for physically disabled students for easy access into buildings. There have been instances where a physically disabled student got to the foot of the steps and had to wait for some charitable students to come along and lift her up with her chair into the room to receive lectures. If a disabled individual cannot go in and out of the lecture room at will then she does not have the same opportunity as her normal counterparts. In some campuses, there are no levelled paved walkways from building to building which would enable a person with a wheelchair to mobilize herself without difficulty or someone on crutches to move easily without her crutches being caught in rough pathways. I once heard a cry from a frustrated student in a higher institution of learning as he was trying to make his way through a walkway just covered with gravel: 'Oh, I wish these gravels were not put here and the pathway left untarred. Everytime I put down my crutches, they get caught in the gravel. I cannot just balance myself. This pathway should either be tarred or cleared of these gravels'. The student was perfectly right. If, as he said, there are unpaved areas of gravel which obstruct wheelchair movement or hinder the use of walking aids, equal opportunity demands that there be paved areas to allow disabled people a free environment to move around the institution.

Considering the infrastructures of some of the institutions — high raised buildings where some classrooms are on the second or third floors or the Academic and Student Affairs offices are above the first floor — lifts or escalators must be provided for those in wheelchairs to have access into these buildings. In most of the developing countries, where disabled individuals studying in institutions of higher learning are still a novelty, these provisions are absent because the buildings were not erected with them in mind. Therefore, higher education for individuals like these becomes extremely difficult and in some cases impossible. Equal opportunity in education would demand a conducive environment for these people to learn. Of equal importance are the doors into the classrooms and the toilets which must be wide enough to provide free passage. They should in no way pose a problem for those using either crutches or wheelchairs.

Blind People

In Nigeria, like the orthopaedically disabled, blind people take their examinations like other normal individuals but in braille form. Unlike the orthopaedically handicapped whose learning mode is like that of other able-bodied students, blind peoples' mode of reading and writing is different. They require certain equipment not required by normal students. In place of a pen, they need a braille machine. In terms of cost, the difference is great. A biro pen may cost ₦ 1 while a braille machine would cost between ₦ 2,500 to ₦ 3,000 and a typewriter would cost between ₦ 600 to ₦ 1,000. In place of eyesight, they use their hearing modality, and hence need a tape recorder to tape their lectures. This equipment is very important to blind people and must be made available to them. It is important too that money should be provided for batteries or that sockets be provided in the classrooms where they can use the power current. Whereas a sighted student gets books ready from the bookshop, the work of blind people is only beginning when they get their books from the bookshop. They now have the tedious job of having the books transcribed into braille form or on recorded cassettes by volunteer readers.

This is not to say that nothing is being done. There are some institutions such as the University of Jos which has made some progress in providing the necessary facilities. There is a resource room which is well equipped in terms of equipment and staff. There is a full-time braille technician who transcribes inkprint materials for blind students and makes tactile materials for them. Also, the prisoners' services are being fully utilized. They have been trained to write braille so they can transcribe textbooks, etc. for blind students. The University of Jos Department of Special Education also organizes volunteer readers to read for them and also to tape books and materials for them.

Furthermore, credit should be given to some philanthropic organizations who have taken it on themselves to assist the various institutions of the disabled in terms of equipment and teaching materials. Among these are the International Soroptimist Club of Lagos. Many institutions of the blind in Nigeria have benefited from their generosity. Equipment such as tape recorders, typewriters and blank cassettes have been supplied for the use of blind students. Arrangements are also on the way to setting up a braille press in Lagos.

Another organization that needs to be mentioned is the Christoffel Blinden Mission (CBM) whose contribution to the welfare of blind people is also great. It has not only supplied equipment but funds for feeding. One such Centre that has benefited from them is St. Joseph's Centre for Blind People in Obudu in Cross River State. Another organization that has contributed greatly in the welfare of the disabled in Nigeria is the Rotary Club of Nigeria. They have contributed equipment to the various institutions of learning for the use of disabled students and also awarded a number of scholarships to disabled students in Nigeria. Furthermore, a major contribution is the partial funding of the Early Preventive Immunisation (EPI) programme. This programme was launched nationwide on 26 October 1984 by Major General Mohammed Buhari to combat the deadly diseases of childhood — polio, measles, tuberculosis, tetanus, whooping cough and diphtheria. In discussing the EPI programme, UNICEF needs to be mentioned. This organization has played a major role in the implementation of this programme, contributing equipment and supplies. The World Health Organisation has likewise contributed in eradicating these diseases, thus contributing to the prevention of various disabilities in Nigeria.

However, in spite of these efforts, there is still much to be done to improve the condition of disabled people in our institutions of learning. Until such time as Government makes these necessary facilities — braille machines, typewriters, braille technicians — available free of charge to the students in our institutions of learning to enhance their success, I would say that equal opportunity is not fully a reality in either the Nigerian situation or any other nation with similar problems.

Apart from equipment and manpower, there is also the question of a safe environment. For example, if there are broken windows and doors that would constitute a safety hazard for blind people, who 'see' with their hands, there is no opportunity for exploration. If there are objects protruding into the path of circulation such as air convectors, which people with visual impairments might bump into because they cannot see them or locate them with their canes, such an environment does not provide free opportunity of movement. Until such objects are removed, raised or marked to allow blind people free passage, I would say there is no equal opportunity given them for learning or movement, nor opportunity for exploration and discovery.

An important aspect of equal opportunity in the education of blind people would be the provision of a braille press where books can be provided for braille readers. Nigeria is in the process of getting one which would serve blind people throughout the Federation. Until a braille press is in operation, we need to develop some interim measure to deal with the difficulties. One immediate way of solving our problem of braille materials is to train a group of people as braille specialists and employ them in various centres in the States or Local Governments. All materials such as examination question papers, required readings in the schools, etc. would be brought to these Centres for fast transcribing. This practice is already in operation in some States in Nigeria.

Deaf People

Deaf people are a group who, because of the nature of their

disability not being visible on first sight, are generally disregarded. They also need equal opportunity to get a high education and to gain knowledge.

Deaf people get information through the language of signs, lip reading and finger spelling. Most often a lecturer, not deliberately, but through ignorance may decide to walk round the lecture room as she lectures or as she writes on the chalkboard. Deaf students are then not able to catch the movement of her lips and facial expression through which they obtain most of their information. Deaf students are then denied the opportunity of acquiring information. In some advanced countries where equal opportunity has become a reality, there are government funds made available for deaf students to employ interpreters. This is very important. It is something that needs to be provided for in the education of those with hearing impediments.

Equal Opportunity

Furthermore, in-service courses could be given to teachers to familiarize them on how various disabled people acquire knowledge. Until the points raised in this chapter are fully implemented, equal opportunity in education for disabled people in Nigeria and most other developing countries is still by and large not a reality and is to some extent a myth.

One may ask whether equality of opportunity means identical treatment. Not so. Equality does not mean identical treatment. The crucial value to be fostered by our system of education is the opportunity given to everyone to succeed. Undoubtedly, while all are equal under the law, nature and circumstances yield advantage to some while handicapping others. Therefore, to say we are offering children equal opportunity in education while at the same time disregarding differences in their circumstances is merely to maintain or perhaps even magnify the relative effects of advantage and handicap. Furthermore, Subsection (c) of Section (55) states that the aim is:

> To provide opportunities for exceptionally gifted children to develop at their own pace in the interest of the Nation's economic and technological development.

In practice this aspect of the policy is still in its rudimentary stage.

Gifted People

In 1986, the Federal Ministry of Education set up a Committee to work out strategies for the identification and nurturing of gifted individuals in the country. Half a million naira were set aside for the programme. This was a step in the right direction. It was an indication that the time has finally arrived in Nigeria to stop the wasting of talent. So far, subcommittees have also been set up in the various States and some Resource persons have developed various tests in readiness for identification. Nevertheless, there is still a lot to be done if success is to be achieved. After the gifted individuals have been identified, there has to be arrangement for their education. They can be educated in a number of ways. They can be provided for in the regular school setting through enrichment programmes. In this case, well equipped libraries and laboratories are very important. Although there are some very good libraries in some States of the Federation, there are also libraries and laboratories which are far from adequate. Another approach is to establish a few special schools and classes for the gifted, but this too has not taken off. However, the University of Calabar has been identified as a Centre of excellence as regards the gifted. Here, teachers of the gifted would be trained in the identification and nurturing of the gifted. What is of great importance and urgency is to establish an Assessment Centre or Centres in the country where children suspected to be very talented or gifted could be referred for comprehensive assessment, and if found to be really gifted would be recommended for placement, and hence his/her giftedness nurtured.

Integration

The Nigerian Policy on Education points out an important aspect of Special Education. This is the aspect of integration which has been a much debated issue in recent times. It states: 'Integration is the most realistic form of Special Education since handicapped children are expected to live in the society'. The Policy states that special classes and units will be provided in the ordinary schools and that, when necessary, special schools will be established.

University level — change of attitude

There is no doubt that great progress has been made in the country in establishing special schools. In almost every State of the twenty-one States in the Federation, there is a special school. In most of the States there are schools for people who are blind, deaf and orthopaedically handicapped and in some States, schools for people who are mentally retarded. What is vital now is to improve on the quality of the services obtained in these institutions. They need to be adequately equipped in terms of materials and personnel. Also, since integration has been endorsed by the Federal Government of Nigeria, Special Resource Centres need to be established in the various States to service a number of schools run by a Local Government.

In terms of personnel development, a lot of progress has been made towards this as contained in the policy. The Commonwealth Societies for Blind and for Deaf people have for a number of years awarded overseas scholarships to Nigerian nationals in the effort to develop work opportunities for them in Nigeria. Most of the Nigerian pioneers of Special Education benefited from these scholarships. Two universities — Ibadan and Jos — offer degree, diploma and certificate programmes in Special Education. There are also Units in various Faculties of Education in a number of Universities offering Special Education courses. In addition to this, there is an Advance Teachers College of Special Education. This offers the Nigerian Certificate of Education in Special Education. The Nigerian Government for a long time now have sponsored people to go into the field of Special Education by offering scholarships to individuals both within and outside the country. Some of us have benefited from this offer. In this respect, Nigeria should allow herself a little measure of congratulation but nevertheless should not lose heart that the journey is only beginning. As stated in Subsection (4) of Section (55), all Teachers' Training Colleges will provide general and special education to all prospective teachers who would be teaching in normal schools but who require such knowledge to identify and help handicapped children. This is being implemented by the Government, and now elements of Special Education are being introduced in all Teachers' Colleges to give the regular class teachers rudimentary education in Special Education.

Of importance too is the Government's Policy on Employment. Subsection (8) of the policy states that Government will provide suitable employment opportunities for handicapped workers and that sheltered workshops will be established for those handicapped individuals who may not be able to work in open industries. Like everyone else, the majority of handicapped persons here are finding it difficult to get jobs. It is very important to have placement officers in the various States to enable disabled persons who have successfully completed their training programmes to get jobs. An aspect which must not be overlooked is that of legislation to protect disabled people. Many third world countries, including Nigeria, do not have legislation to protect their disabled population. Even where such legislation has been made, there is a discrepancy between legislation and practice.

In most industrialized nations, there is legislation to protect the rights of disabled people, such as the right to an appropriate education in the least restricted environment (PL 94-142), the right of way and the right to employment. Legislation which gives disabled people such protection needs to be enacted and practised in Nigeria. In 1981, however, the Plateau State of Nigeria passed the *Handicapped Education Law,* giving disabled persons in the State the right to an appropriate education. Some States in the Federation have passed similar laws. This law I believe would be more effective if made on the National level rather than left to individual States. Such a move would entitle the handicapped person, irrespective of place of origin, to obtain education and Government financial assistance wherever he resides in the country.

Finally, a very serious omission in the policy is the provision of pre-school programmes and support programmes for parents of handicapped infants aged 0-7. The pre-school period is a very important period for character formation and learning, and when handicapped children are not helped to grow up in the right manner, it becomes more difficult. Of importance is the sort of support parents need from professionals, such as parent counselling programmes. These need to be provided for the children and parents if the proper development of the children is to be attained.

Of importance also is the matter of a census of disabled people in the country. This is a very important point in the policy, but unfortunately it is still more of a theory than practice. The key to success in the care of the disabled is to know the population one is planning to serve. The allocation of Government funds and development of programmes depend on the knowledge of the population to be served.

Factors Militating Against Implementation of the Policy

There are many factors militating against the implementation of this policy on Special Education. As stated above, there is a phenomenon common among the third world countries which is the fact that heroic and noble ideas are generally written on paper but rarely do they become a reality. One reason for this unfortunate situation is the fact that they are all suffering from one common 'disease' which is *poverty*. Many of these ideas will only see the light of day if there are funds available to implement them. *Secondly,* there is the lack of conviction about the rights of the disabled persons. It is not uncommon to hear people say, 'We have not even finished providing for the able-bodied, why do you think we should bother about the disabled?', suggesting that disabled people are only to be catered for after all the needs of the able ones have been met. *Thirdly,* there is the question of manpower development. In most places, there are no qualified staff to implement the programmes proposed. Without good, dedicated members of staff, the situation can be likened to trying to catch fish in the deep sea with bare hands. *Fourthly,* another problem that plagues developing nations, particularly African nations, is *nepotism,* or *tribalism* as it is generally known. This comes into play when one in power wants only someone from his tribe to occupy a certain position irrespective of whether there is a more qualified person than the one being given the post. As a result, it is not uncommon to find someone who has less qualifications being head of a Unit, with more qualified persons under him.

Recommendations

From the discussion above, it is evident that in the Nigerian situation, like that of many other nations, there exists a discrepancy between policies and practice. The Nigerian Policy on Education as it affects special education is still inadequate.

It is relevant that the following points made in the Policy be seen to as a matter of urgency:
(1) A census of the number of disabled and gifted people in the country must be taken.
(2) There is a need for early identification and for pre-school programmes to be established.
(3) There is need for the development of manpower in the field and for adequate funding of Special Education programmes.

(4)   There is the need to enact laws to protect the handicapped — *The Three Rights* as I would prefer to term it: the right to an appropriate education; the right to free movement; and the right to employment.

It is hoped that if these recommendations are implemented, the gap between policy and practice as regards the National Policy on Special Education will be narrowed.

References

ABANG, T.B. 'Provision for Special Education in the New National Policy on Education'. Unpublished paper presented at Campus Seminar on the Role of Universities and the New National Policy on Education, June 1987, University of Jos.

KIRK, S. (1979) *Exceptional Children*, Boston, Houghton Mifflin Company.

NIGERIAN NATIONAL POLICY ON EDUCATION (1977), revised (1981).

PUBLIC LAW 94-142 OF THE UNITED STATES OF AMERICA (1975).

Chapter 7

Residential Homes for Physically Disabled Adults: Lessons from the present and potential for the future

Jan Goodall

Introduction

The best known English work on this topic, *A Life Apart* (Miller & Gwynne, 1972) has had considerable influence, and there has been much progress towards good practice in residential work since it was written. However, several writers have recently drawn attention to the continuing inadequacies of residential homes as long term settings for people with physical disabilities (Comerford, 1986; MacFarlane, 1987; Leat, 1988). This chapter reports some of the findings of a case study of one purpose built residential establishment which makes every effort to minimize the detrimental effects of institutional living.

Upper Springland, Perth, is administered by the Scottish Council for Spastics, a voluntary organization which employs about 700 people in three special schools, three residences for adults and two sheltered workshops/day centres. In the early 1970s the Scottish Council believed that further residential provision for its adult clients was urgently needed. In Scotland there were no Local Authority hostels for disabled people, there had been no building programme for hospital Younger Disabled Living Units, such as had taken place in England, and there were only a few homes run by voluntary organizations. Some of these operated with an upper age limit, and there were no places into which the older residents could move.

Members and officers of the Scottish Council for Spastics made attempts to research the latest advances in the field — they studied the Fokus Society's flats in Sweden and the large disabled people's village in Holland, Het Dorp. (See Lancaster-Gaye, 1972) In common with most service providers at that time they do not seem to have questioned the 'traditional assumption that people must move into residential establishments if they need regular help with daily routines and cannot assure it through an able family' (Shearer, 1982). It was thought that the ideal solution would be to create several small units in different parts of Scotland, but lack of money made this impossible. Personal contacts then resulted in an offer by the Gannochy Trust of a five acre site beside the river Tay at Perth and a grant of £500,000 for building costs. Such a generous offer could not be refused by a voluntary organization with very limited funds, but accepting it had certain far-reaching consequences. Firstly, there was no possibility of adopting the Fokus model, providing accommodation for disabled people integrated with mainstream housing, because the money had been given 'to help disabled people'. Secondly, because the site was about a mile by road from the centre of town and about three quarters of a mile from the nearest shops, there was an inherent danger of creating a segregated disabled community. So it happened that the Scottish Council for Spastics found itself concentrating resources in one geographical area, on one isolated site and initially with plans to provide accommodation for seventy-two disabled residents. (This was later modified to fifty-one residents with another twelve places for respite care.) Management, residents and staff are still having to cope with the inevitable drawbacks created by the establishment's location and size. The complex was developed in three phases as Figure 1 shows.

It was originally intended to offer permanent accommodation for adults who were disabled to the extent that they required some help with activities of daily living, but who were mentally and emotionally capable of running their own lives. This intention is reflected in the regime which is still in operation at Upper Springland — staff do not enter residents' flats unless they have been invited in, or the resident has called for help by using the pager. Thus the resident is expected to exercise judgement in making his or her needs known. This way of life suits many of the residents very well indeed; however, it creates some problems for staff in a few cases when a resident's ability to take responsibility for himself seems questionable.

The Research Project

In 1985 the Scottish Council for Spastics approached the University

Figure 1: Upper Springland: Phases of Development

Phase 1 *1978*	24 Flatlets with central kitchen/servery, dining rooms and lounges. Workshop adjacent.
Phase 2 *1982*	24 Flatlets with central servery, dining rooms and lounges. New central kitchen, foyer with bar. Offices.
Phase 3 *1987*	Holiday/Respite Care Unit – 12 beds. 'Small' Unit – 3 beds. Community Centre with theatre/sports hall, meeting rooms and kitchen. Hydrotherapy pool and gymnasium. Workshop (now 'Skill Centre') extended. Workshop staff organize activities for residents and about 20 day attenders.

Each resident has a self-contained bed sitting room with its own shower and toilet, and a front door opening onto a street-like corridor. All meals are provided and attendant care is available 24 hours per day.

of Dundee with proposals for a two year study of the changing needs of the residents and the changing activities of the staff at Upper Springland.

During the ten years since the first phase opened, a change had taken place in the nature of the demand for places. Local authorities and housing associations were providing increasing numbers of houses suitable for disabled people, and many of the early residents had moved out into the community. People who were capable of running their own lives were only applying if they were very severely disabled indeed — requiring total care in all aspects of daily life. Applicants were now being put forward for admission who were less severely physically disabled, but who had other difficulties such as a long history of institutionalization, borderline mental handicap, epilepsy, poor mental health or behavioural problems. Thus the original concept of Upper Springland was already being called in question. Even with increased staffing levels, Upper Springland could only accept a limited number of residents who needed total care, and there was concern about the demands and stresses placed on the largely untrained care staff in working with people who needed a lot of emotional support or who lacked motivation. The Scottish Council for Spastics believed that in this situation of change an in-depth research study of the establishment's functioning would assist them in planning for its future.

Two main groups of research questions were identified. Firstly, what is the establishment for? What were its original objectives, how have these changed since the first phase opened and how should they be developed in the future? This included consideration of the potential contribution of Upper Springland to the spectrum of services in Scotland. Secondly, what are the internal and external factors which constrain or facilitate the establishment's functioning? A variety of research methods were used and Figure 2 lists the sources of information on which the research findings are based.

Figure 2: Sources of Information

1 Formal and informal observation in the public areas at Upper Springland.
2 Informal conversations with residents and staff.
3 Meetings of residents and staff.
4 Reading documents at Upper Springland and Headquarters.
5 Confidential, semi-structured, tape recorded individual interviews with residents and staff.
6 Additional interviews with senior management, unit leaders and heads of staff departments.

Management and almost all the residents and members of staff welcomed the project, which had been carefully explained to them before it began. 91 per cent of residents and 91 per cent of staff agreed to take part in the individual interviews. The answers to the interview questions were coded and analyzed using the micro computer data base program 'Reflex', but much of the information consisted of expressions of feelings and ideas which are liable to shift and may not fit readily into coding schemes. Moreover the subject of the research was a living system. Changes were constantly taking place during the main field work period (August 1986–April 1987), and many more will have taken place since then. No claim is made to have discovered 'the truth' about Upper Springland, but a number of interesting themes emerged from the study, and a selection of these are outlined below. Because of space limitations we are confined here to a general description of the regime and discussion of the needs and aspirations of the residents. Aspects of the interviews with staff will be reported separately.

Some Research Findings

We were interested in obtaining the residents' view of how they came to be living at Upper Springland, so they were asked why they had applied and where they had been living previously. Only 28 per cent said they had come from domestic settings — their parents' or other relatives' homes. The largest group (37 per cent) had been living in other residential establishments. Of the remainder, 16 per cent had come from mental handicap hospitals, 12 per cent from general hospitals and 7 per cent from residential schools or colleges. Thus for many people admission to Upper Springland represented a move from one institution to another which was expected to offer a better way of life. No one said that any alternative living arrangements had been considered; this reflects accurately the fact that in Scotland there has been no range of options available to disabled people and few challenges to the paternalist assumptions of service providers. The situation in England and Wales is much the same (Fiedler, 1988).

Three quarters of the residents (74 per cent) said that they found their present way of life at Upper Springland compared favourably with their previous living arrangements, and our observations and information about the way of life at Upper Springland give some indication of the reasons for this.

The Way of Life

The Officer in Charge and the Depute Officer in Charge (Care), who were both qualified Social Workers, shared a strong belief that disabled adults should be enabled to live as full and as 'normal' a life as possible, with maximum physical and emotional independence. They were very much aware that Upper Springland had become a large and complex organization; every effort was made to minimize any potentially detrimental effects on the lives of residents by avoiding rigid routines and treating residents as individuals, each with their own unique needs and preferences. Much emphasis was placed on providing a stimulating environment, and staff of all designations were encouraged to chat with residents, and to participate in their recreational and social activities. They were expected to share with the management a commitment to providing a good quality of life both in the material environment of the complex and in its human relationships. They were selected for employment with this in mind, and served a three months' initial probation period, during which their attitude to the residents was a crucial consideration.

The atmosphere was deliberately non-clinical, indeed it was almost anti-clinical. Tending was believed to be mainly a matter of informed common sense, guided by the twin values of respect for individuals and enhancement of independence. Although there were qualified nurses on the staff, no one was working as such, and the district nursing service came in to work with residents if necessary. Upper Springland aimed to provide assistance in activities of daily living such as a disabled person might receive from a relative at home. But the senior officers also believed that disabled people 'ought' to develop their full potential for emotional and physical independence. This belief, combined with the fact that a large proportion of the residents had previously had little opportunity for independence, led to the practice of holding meetings with individual residents to establish goals with them, and to work out ways in which the goals might be met. There was thus a basic discrepancy between the ideal of providing a setting where disabled people could be enabled to live 'normal' lives and the approach to residents as clients, who ought to be helped to change in certain ways assumed to be beneficial.

Reviews

The management aimed to hold discussions with new residents a few weeks after they arrived, then after six months' residence, and thereafter to hold a review meeting once a year. In practice this did not always happen, and one or two residents opted out. One man said he had never had a review because he did not feel the need for one. He said he had rebelled against a lot of things, including the reviews, and this was accepted by the staff. Others did not opt out, but questioned the value of the meetings. One young man hit the nail on the head by saying — *'It is not really done in the outside world, is it? I do not see why they should have it here. It is a waste of time.'* On the other hand, half of the residents found their review meeting was a positive experience, and this highlights the impossibility of any regime suiting every resident.

Keywork

A keyworker system was operated, so that a member of staff was linked with two or three residents, and was expected to take a special interest in them. Likewise residents were expected to consult their key workers about any difficulties they might have. Two thirds of the residents said this system worked well for them, although some felt they had no need of a key worker. As one person put it: *'It's silly giving me a key worker — I am quite capable'.* The keyworkers, who in conjunction with the residents prepared reports for the review meetings, were supposed to coordinate attempts to meet the goals which were identified. For most residents these goals were in very general terms such as improving reading and writing skills. Only one or two had detailed programmes to follow, for example a routine of morning tasks to perform.

The Programme of Daily Activities

The original Workshop underwent a transformation both in its buildings and in its concept during the period of the research study. At first it was compulsory for residents to attend (although one or two exceptions were made). Later there was a period of some doubt among both residents and staff as to whether residents should be compelled to go. Finally it was openly acknowledged that residents need not go, or might attend part time and some of the older people were treated as 'retired'. We estimated that by the end of the project about ten of the forty-eight residents were taking little or no part in the Skill Centre activities. However, if residents had opted to attend an activity, they were expected to make a commitment to it, and to turn up regularly. The enlarged premises and staff enabled a much wider choice of activities to be offered towards the end of the research and the emphasis was on recreation, education and development of interests — the Skill Centre was no longer seen as a workplace.

Decision Making

The research interviews included questions about decision making at Upper Springland. In theory residents and staff were encouraged to make their views known about the running of the establishment.

In addition to residents' meetings in the units there was a Community Council. Representative residents from each of the units met weekly with the Deputy Officer in Charge to discuss issues of communal life. The effectiveness of this was limited by impaired speech, by lack of experience of committee work and by limited understanding of how to use the opportunity offered. Although this was acknowledged and regretted by the management, there seemed to be no effort to train the Community Councillors in their role, or the residents in how to use their representatives. The Community Councillors did have some real influence on matters of everyday life — e.g. on menus and the appointment of basic grade staff, but it was widely acknowledged that the larger policy decisions rested with the Officer in Charge, subject to financial constraints and the approval of Scottish Council for Spastics Headquarters in Edinburgh. The result was a feeling of some confusion and disillusionment. Everyone was encouraged to believe they had a valid opinion and should contribute by expressing their ideas. Much time was spent in meetings, particularly by staff. Yet ultimately the government of the place was out of their hands and some became frustrated, feeling that many of the meetings were a waste of time. This is typical of the problems which arise when attempts are made to run an open and democratic establishment. The reality is that discussions cannot continue indefinitely, decisions have to be made by someone, and responsibility rests with the boss, who is working within externally imposed financial and policy constraints.

Communal Living

Many people spoke of Upper Springland as a community and senior staff cultivated the idea that each person could contribute to the well-being of all. There was an attempt to reduce the divide between staff and residents and to break down departmental barriers between staff. All staff were expected to relate to residents in a friendly and helpful way. This seemed to be very successful in most cases. As an illustration that rapport with residents was not limited to the care staff, the following quotation is taken from an interview with one of the cooks, who was talking about a very severely disabled young man. *'He was sitting in the kitchen one Sunday afternoon and he started to cry. He said he was just fed up — what was there for him to live for?'* This cook said he had taken the same resident away for a weekend break, although the young man required total care in activities of daily living — washing, dressing, toiletting, transfer from bed to chair, etc. There were many other examples in the research material of involvement and commitment by members of staff completely beyond their ordinary duties.

There was a lot to be said in favour of Upper Springland. There was also, of course, the dark side, and life there had its problems, both for residents and staff. Many people, including the Officer in Charge and Depute, said that the place had become too big. Some of the residents said they were disturbed by the noise, bustle and constant changes which are inevitable when big groups of people are living and working together. The staff establishment had become very large. By the end of the project 107 people were employed, working in three shifts; it was a constant struggle for them to make sure that everyone was kept informed of all the things they needed to know. The place was *not* one big, happy family — there were differences of opinion, and personality clashes as well as friendships.

Residents might become relatively isolated in their flats unless they took the initiative to involve themselves with staff or other residents, or make their own contacts in the town. The research interviews revealed that many of them lacked close personal relationships. All but two said members of their family were very important people in their lives, but only a third had families based in the surrounding areas; some went home or were visited regularly, but most saw their relatives seldom. Some had made friends locally, and some mentioned one or two friends among the residents, with whom they chose to spend time, visiting each other's flats. But one third of the residents said they seldom or never visited other residents' flats. For these people life must have been very much a case of being alone in a crowd. There was one married couple among the residents, and one young man who was engaged to one of the day attenders. Very few of the others implied that they had a sexual partner.

Residents' Disabilities

In attempting to describe the level of disability found among the residents at Upper Springland the usual difficulties were encountered. There are innumerable scales and methods of assessment, none of which is entirely satisfactory. Over two thirds (68 per cent) of the residents had cerebral palsy, and had been disabled all their lives. The rest had suffered accidents (13 per cent) or had other disabling conditions (19 per cent) and most of these had become disabled after experiencing a period of adult life free from handicap. Almost a third had severe speech disabilities and three individuals were deaf or hearing impaired. This mix of residents had considerable implications for the social life within the units. Almost two thirds of the residents used wheelchairs within the complex. In addition, some of those able to walk could only manage short distances and might use a wheelchair to go out.

In order to estimate the residents' need for help with self-care the Barthel Index (Granger *et al,* 1979) was used. On this scale a score of 100 indicates complete independence and we were surprised to find that four of the residents scored 100, while another seven scored 90 or more. Thus almost a quarter of the people living at Upper Springland turned out to have little or no physical disability. However, all but two of these individuals had other difficulties such as epilepsy, memory impairment or poor physical or mental health. (Four residents received in-patient hospital treatment for psychiatric illness during the study period.) At the other end of the scale there were seven residents (16 per cent) who scored less than 30, showing that they were extremely severely disabled.

Another way of approaching the assessment of disability is to look at a person's needs for help in terms of time intervals and number of helpers required. One such method is the Wessex 24 hour chart (Cantrell, Dawson and Glastonbury, 1985). The residential unit leaders were asked to complete a 24 hour care chart for each of their residents who had been interviewed for the research project. This information allowed us to describe the people who lived at Upper Springland in terms of four categories of care needs, as Table 1 shows.

Table 1: Residents' needs for help with daily self care (N = 43)

Total care	21%
A lot of help	28%
Help with 'bits and pieces'	24%
No routine help	27%
	100%

The perception of senior members of staff was that this mix of disabilities enabled the residential units to function. Those who required most help with their physical needs were by and large independent in all other ways, so that when they had been attended to, the staff were free to work with the social and emotional difficulties presented by the less severely physically disabled residents. However, senior staff were aware that some residents were very conscious of these difficulties among their neighbours, found their company unstimulating or at times disturbing, and felt that Upper Springland was becoming a less congenial place in which to live.

In thinking about the objectives of Upper Springland and whether it was fulfilling the residents' needs, we were interested in attempting to estimate residents' potential for succeeding in a less sheltered environment. We identified some characteristics which seemed to us important for survival in an autonomous domestic setting, and we evolved a 'self-sufficiency' index consisting of the following three items:

1) *Responsibility for self-care*
This refers to a person's ability to be aware of his/her own needs, to take responsibility for communicating these needs at suitable times and to use help appropriately. It does *not* imply physical independence.

2) *Ability to relate to people*
We thought that a disabled person living in their own home and relying on others for help would need to have considerable social skills, especially when dealing with new helpers, or coping with unexpected hitches in their structure for coping. In our view these skills are determined more by personality and maturity than by speech ability *per se*.

3) *Emotional state*
Conversations with staff, residents and former residents led us to believe that for severely disabled people to succeed in independent living, psychological factors are probably more important than the ability to perform daily living tasks. Therefore we included in the index a common sense assessment of residents' usual mood in terms of levels of depression, anxiety and irritability.

The residential unit leaders were asked to rate their residents on each of these items and the results are shown in Table 2. The Unit Leaders were of course basing their assessments on observations of people living in a very sheltered setting, and it cannot be assumed that they would show the same characteristics elsewhere. But it seems likely that more than half the residents at Upper Springland had good or

Table 2: 'Self Sufficiency' Index (N = 43)

Responsibility for self care		Emotional State	
Very good	39%	Very good	48%
Good	14%	Good	21%
OK	35%	OK	24%
Poor	5%	Poor	7%
Very poor	7%		100%
	100%		

Ability to relate to people	
Very good	34%
Good	17%
OK	42%
Poor	4%
Very poor	3%
	100%

very good potential for successfully moving out into the community if they wished to do so.

Residents' Opinions and Aspirations

Some of the questions in the interviews with residents were designed to produce a picture of how they felt about life at Upper Springland. Two aspects which were generally appreciated were the opportunities for privacy and for company —

> 'You have got a flat which you can do anything in'
> 'I like the freedom to stay in my flat or go and sit in the common room'

80 per cent of residents said that they found the way they were spending their life these days was either completely satisfying or pretty satisfying. It seems that much of the bad reputation of life in residential homes stems from experience of unsuitable buildings, patronising staff attitudes, rigid routines, lack of privacy and lack of occupation. The research at Upper Springland indicates that even in a large institution it is possible to create a positive atmosphere and to offer an acceptable way of life. However, when the residents were asked whether they would prefer to live alone or with another

Table 3: Would you prefer to live alone or with another person if you could get enough help? (N = 43)

Yes	61%
No	21%
Yes and No	9%
Don't know/No answer	9%
	100%

person if they could get enough help, almost two thirds said that they would. The details of the response to this question are shown in Table 3.

At first sight this finding is in unexpected contrast with the high level of satisfaction with life at Upper Springland which had been expressed. The following observations may throw some light on the matter.

1)   The rather clumsy phrasing of the question was intended to convey interest in how people would like to live *given the reality of their present disability*. This may not have been successful and some of the respondents may actually have been saying that they would prefer not to be disabled.

2)   The question was being posed in the abstract, and not as part of a planning exercise for the resident's future. It was not necessary for them to give serious consideration to the benefits they would lose and the responsibilities they would acquire by leaving Upper Springland.

3)   Most of the residents had no experience of running a household, having lived in their parental homes or in institutions. They may have had limited ideas about what independent living would be like, as was found in a recent study of people living in homes run by the English Spastics Society (Bennion, 1988).

In spite of the above complicating elements in the interpretation of the finding, it seems likely that experience of life at Upper Springland had enabled some people to gain in self-confidence, and to widen their horizons so that they felt ready to move out. As one member of staff put it —

'This environment allows people to mature — they start making their own decisions, leading their own lives. I have seen individuals

outgrowing the place. Although they need the physical help, they don't need the stimulation. There is nothing for them here — they can go it alone, if you like'.

Unfortunately this success in enhancing residents' independence was not matched by any established scheme for helping residents to 'go it alone' — there was no member of staff with this specific remit. The policy was to offer people a home for life — there was neither an age limit nor a limit to the length of time people might stay. It was usually left up to the resident to initiate any plans to move on. Perhaps if staff had taken the initiative it would have seemed to them as though they were rejecting the residents — conveying a message that they had outstayed their welcome. It is questionable whether staff can devote their energies to providing the best possible quality of life within the unit and simultaneously wrestle with the practical and emotional challenges of helping people to leave residential care.

Conclusion

In their enthusiasm for integrated living, some leaders of the disabled people's movement seem to believe that there should be no future for residential homes. The case study reported here does support the view that many disabled people are living in such establishments because they have no alternative, and not because they need the degree of staff support and protection which is offered. But it would be unjustified to conclude that there is no legitimate role for residential homes.

The Wagner Report (1988) suggests that 'residential care should be an option for people with physical handicaps, but always in the context of a flexible range of alternatives'. No doubt there are pros and cons to all the alternatives. For people who rely on others for help in performing the tasks of daily living, independent life is far from easy. Some of the reasons for this stem from social factors which could be changed given the political will. But other problems are inherent — a carefully worked out structure for coping is always vulnerable. Inevitably the unexpected happens and things go wrong from time to time. Not all disabled people have the self-confidence, drive, commitment, emotional stability and physical health which are required to face these uncertainties. Some may prefer to take an easier course and settle for communal living with guaranteed access to help.

The views of the residents at Upper Springland who expressed no wish to move on are just as important as the aspirations of those who would prefer to live elsewhere. The trend towards integrated living should not blind us to the fact that we still have a sizeable population of people disabled from birth who have never thought of themselves as householders. For them, 'Independent Living does not involve the embracing of a "normal", or "ordinary" lifestyle, but rather one which is very unfamiliar' (Bennion, 1988) The current demand for integrated schooling and Conductive Education indicates that parents are now seeking maximum independence for their handicapped children. But until recently disabled young people in Britain have been taught to expect lifelong dependency, and for the next few decades there will continue to be some who require traditional protective services, including residential care. We must ensure that they are offered the best possible quality of life and Upper Springland provides a demonstration that communal living need not produce apathy or misery.

Perhaps the most interesting finding of the case study is the evidence that this institution was actually helping to deinstitutionalize some people. Opportunities for personal growth were offered which some residents were able to use to the full, so that they moved from emotional dependency to a state of maturity and ability to direct their own lives. This suggests that residential homes may have a useful function as transitional settings — firstly for adults who wish to break free from dependency; secondly for young people who because of disability may need more than average support in leaving their parental homes; and thirdly for newly disabled adults who may need time and help to adjust to their situation after leaving hospital.

For such a remit to be successful, it will be necessary to establish reliable systems for helping people to move out of residential care into the community without 'reinventing the wheel' each time it is done; and of course we must continue to press both for Wagner's flexible range of available alternatives and for a barrier free society.

Notes

1 This chapter is adapted from a paper presented at the conference on Disability Handicap and Policy held at Bristol Polytechnic in July, 1988.
2 The research project was conceived and supervised by Professor E.L.G. Mapstone who also took part in the data collection. It was funded for two years by the Scottish Home and Health Department.
3 Thanks are due to all those who made this work possible — the officers

and staff of the Scottish Council for Spastics, the residents at Upper Springland and Mrs Agnes Ramsay, research secretary.

References

BENNION, C. (1988) *Choosing to Live Independently,* London, Spastics Society.

CANTRELL, T., DAWSON, J. and GLASTONBURY, G. (1985) *Prisoners of Handicap,* London, RADAR.

COMERFORD, S. (1986a) 'Reasons to be cheerful . . .', *Community Care,* 4 December, pp. 18-9.

COMERFORD, S. (1986b) 'Waiting for a cup of tea', *Community Care,* 11 December, pp. 24-5.

FIEDLER, B. (1988a) 'A fair slice of the cake', *Community Care,* 4 February, pp. 30-1.

FIEDLER, B. (1988b) *Living Options Lottery: Housing and Support Services for people with severe physical disabilities, 1986/88,* London, The Prince of Wales' advisory group on disability.

GRANGER, C.V., ALBRICHT, G. and HAMILTON, B. (1979) 'Outcome of Comprehensive Medical Rehabilitation: Measurement by PULSES Profile and the BARTHEL Index', *Archives of Physical Medicine Rehabilitation,* Vol. 60, pp. 145-54.

LANCASTER-GAYE, D. (1972) *Personal Relationships: the Handicapped and the Community,* London, Routledge & Kegan Paul.

LEAT, D. (1988) 'Younger Physically Disabled Adults' in *Residential Care: The Research Reviewed,* Literature Surveys commissioned by the Independent Review of Residential Care, London, National Institute for Social Work/HMSO.

MACFARLANE, A. (1987) 'Open up the channels of communication', *Social Work Today,* 18 May, p.11.

MILLER, E.J. and GWYNNE, G.V. (1972) *A Life Apart: A Pilot Study of Residential Institutions for the Physically Handicapped and the Young Chronic Sick,* London, Tavistock.

SHEARER, A. (1982) *Living Independently,* London, Centre on Environment for the Handicapped and King Edward's Hospital Fund for London.

WAGNER, G. (1988) *Residential Care, A Positive Choice.* (Report of the Independent Review of Residential Care) London, National Institute for Social Work/HMSO.

Chapter 8

Beyond Integration Policy —
The Deconstruction of Disability

Jan Branson and Don Miller

'Disability', 'handicap', 'policy' — they fit together like pieces of a jigsaw puzzle, or, more correctly, they flow into one another, feed off each other, reinforcing each other, essential ingredients in a distinctly Western, distinctly capitalist mode of thought. The 'disabled', a marginalized group whose failures to satisfy the culturally-specific, historically-specific standards of physical or behavioural 'normality', display 'handicaps', inabilities to deal 'effectively', as individuals, with life in Western capitalist society, their 'handicaps' demanding, in the eyes of those for whom they are an 'other', *a* 'policy', an objective, clearly-formulated, bureaucratically-realizable, logical, coherent approach to dealing with/coping with, their 'handicaps'. The policy demands a 'programme' to transform the policy into practice through effective 'administration'. 'Segregation' was/is such a policy. 'Integration' is another version of the same, another sibling of the triad — disability, handicap, policy — a policy spawning programmes designed in terms of the demands of effective administration.

This chapter challenges conventional notions of/assumptions about policy, integration policy in particular. Through a thorough theorizing of the construction and reproduction of disabilities in Western capitalist societies it challenges the very mode of thought, the very cosmology, that shapes our view of humanity and our place in nature. We conclude that Integration must be a policy/programme oriented towards its own constant destruction; a policy that denies the possibility of a policy, that refuses to submit/subordinate the lives, the sensibilities, the identities of people to a singular/unitary programme; that rejects the demands of a logocentric, unitary administration.

Our critical appraisal of integration policy, developed through the praxis of ongoing empirical research, explores the need, the possibility for the effective deconstruction/destruction of the categories of integration/segregation. Contemporary 'deconstruction theory' (itself an anomaly since 'deconstruction theory' demands its own deconstruction and thus the denial of its categorical existence), particularly as manifested in the work of Gayatri Chakravorty Spivak (1987), provides the basis for an effective exploration first of the processes by which notions such as 'normality'/'abnormality', 'able-bodied'/'disabled' are constructed, and second of the part such categorical thinking plays in the reproduction of capitalist society. Particular attention is given to the vital importance, in the development of this conceptual apparatus basic to discrimination against those deemed 'disabled', of the triumph of a politically innocuous, mechanistic, unitary and phallogocentric science over its more spiritualist, non-unitary and radical opponents in the sixteenth century.

In the search for a theory adequate to the task of understanding the policy/aspiration 'integration', we have, as a matter of course and not simply because of the dearth of theorizing on the disabled, considered the applicability of theories dealing with other marginalized populations. Two particularly provocative theoretical discourses are of particular relevance: of course Foucault's discussion of the birth of the clinic, but even more so, recent feminist theory which searches for an understanding of sexism through the deconstruction of contemporary texts, revealing the intricacies of meaning construction and uncovering the mode of thought that organises 'reality', that appropriates and devalues 'others' — packaging, labelling, controlling — unitary, logocentric, phallogocentric, in its orientation. The feminism of Gayatri Chakravorty Spivak challenges us at every turn to transcend and move beyond a narrow unitary frame of mind, to read 'against the grain', to develop alternative political strategies. As Kristeva (see Moi, 1986) refuses to be bound by *a* feminism or Strathern (1985) to be contained by/within a 'feminist anthropology', so Spivak rejects the suffocating unitary frameworks that bind thought and action — literary, political, sexual . . . Her deconstruction of text, of the academy, is the deconstruction of Western society as a whole and of a Western mode of thought that extends well beyond the confines of Western society, an epistemic imperialism.

Our theorizing has thus rejected the confines of disciplines, of 'special ed.', 'the sociology of education', or 'social policy', to link up with the most vital current debates about culture and society, about base and superstructure, about ideology, about the processes of marginalization and discrimination. We will show that to deconstruct 'integration'/'segregation', 'the disabled', or 'the handicapped' is to deconstruct the entire socio-cultural fabric in the same way as Spivak's deconstruction of the academy reveals the ruthless discriminatory contours of the wider society and Iragaray's deconstruction of gender lays bare the prejudices of a phallogocentric society. The deconstruction of integration is the deconstruction of capitalist society — its ideology, its culture, its very mode of thought, the contours of its habitus, the bases for its practice, its history. Truly radical integration programmes, those oriented to their own destruction, challenge the entire socio-economic order of capitalism, revealing its inherent contradictions and thus promoting its transformation.

In this chapter, we seek not only to trace the historical process whereby 'the disabled' were created, but claim that this process was central to the development of capitalism — the ideological linchpin in the whole process of capitalist development. Its import lies not so much in the development of an ethic of compulsion to work (cf. Abberley, 1987, p. 17) but in the development of a particular approach to the person, the individual, central to the legal/political identity of *all participants* in capitalist production — employers and employees alike.

The vital importance of the ideology of 'disabilities' in Western society is related to the establishment of an 'essentialist' ideology as integral to the development of capitalism. The suffering of the disabled, the most extreme victims of essentialist ideology in Western society, is an ideological practice which lies at the very heart of capitalist ideology as the embodiment of the 'other', the negativity, against which capitalism realises its aims.

Before we explore the nature of this essentialist ideology further, a note on the identity of 'the disabled'. Abberley points to the vast range and number of 'impaired' persons. In this chapter we focus on those who were until recently, or who still are, segregated, kept apart from the rest of society, those for whom separate institutions have been established. We refer to those whose 'abnormality' is not partial but total. These are the people who provide the acid test for Integration. These are the people who are ideologically most vital, who are the embodiment of the 'other' in a world ideologically dependent on 'normality'. Others less 'impaired' but none-the-less deemed disabled are 'touched' by the abnormality embodied in the institutionalized, those shut away — out of sight, out of mind — but essential to capitalist ideology, a vital negativity. These are the people who do not just need technological assistance to make them 'as normal as possible', whose so-called 'disability' is intangible, non-sensible, unavailable to the five senses, whose 'disability' cannot be understood mechanistically but only in terms of syndromatic pictures of 'normal' 'abnormality' based on observed behaviour patterns. These are the 'cerebral palsied', the 'autistic', the 'Downs syndrome kids' . . . They defy the clinical gaze. *They do not fit* in the scientists' law-governed, ordered nature. They defy capitalist/ 'scientific' cosmology. Once the treatment of these 'severely disabled' is understood, the theory can move to consider the way the ideology influences the lives of others. It casts its shadow over some and illuminates the lives of others.

Theorizing the Ideological Foundations of 'The Disabled'

Theorizing essentialism, Western thought's fundamental dependence on a unitary subject, its humanism, its logocentrism, has been the particular concern of post-structuralism, of theories focusing on the decoding, the deconstruction of language — the texts of our culture. Weedon (1987) sums up the position well:

> The terms *subject* and *subjectivity* are central to poststructuralist theory and they mark a crucial break with humanist conceptions of the individual which are still central to Western philosophy and political and social organization . . . Humanist discourses presuppose an essence at the heart of the individual which is unique, fixed and coherent and which makes her what she *is.* . . . Against this irreducible humanist essence of subjectivity, poststructuralism proposes a subjectivity which is precarious, contradictory and in process, constantly being reconstituted in discourse each time we think or speak.
>
> The political significance of decentering the subject and abandoning the belief in essential subjectivity is that it opens up subjectivity to change. (pp. 32-3)

The exploration of the way subjectivity is interpolated for the 'disabled', this exploration of the ideological roots of our culture is therefore an overtly political project. Just as 'feminist interests have placed subjectivity, signifying practices and sexuality on the theoretical agenda' (p.12) in order to deal with the political issues central to the fight against sexism, the interests of the disabled must at least as urgently place subjectivity, signifying practices and sexuality — understood following Foucault (1981) as the discursive constitution of the body — on theirs, revealing the way their interests converge and diverge with and from those of others 'subjected' to discriminatory treatment.

But before proceeding further with our investigation of essentialist ideology, we must not be tempted to treat it in isolation. While language is the site for the construction of subjectivity, the social consequences of this subjectivity are experienced in relationships, in unequal relationships where inequalities are far from random but structured, enduring through time, through generations in terms of class, race, ethnicity, gender *and* the experience of a subjectivity 'disabled'. In the reproduction of these structured social inequalities the interweaving of economic, political, cultural and ideological factors is complex and the source of much controversy. While they are expressed through culture and conceptualized ideologically the ultimate site of their construction remains the subject of present debate. Do such inequalities all ultimately serve economic ends? Does the mode of production — the articulation of the forces and relations of production — determine the form of all social relations, the 'base', the cake, underlying the superstructure, the icing, of the political, juridicial, ideological/cultural?

It was Marx who stressed that theory must not only be oriented towards understanding the world but to changing it. It was also Marx who stressed the central importance of the relations of production, of the material conditions of existence in the construction of class-based inequalities. It is Marx who is also identified (in many ways unfairly) with the devaluation of ideology and culture as sites for revolutionary action, giving rise to a general scorn among many revolutionary theorists for theorizing these so-called 'superstructural' elements. But the last two decades have seen a reevaluation of theoretical priorities which lay a firm theoretical base for our overtly political project. Marxist feminists in particular have left such 'vulgar materialism' far behind to show that while the economy exploits the cultural differentiation male/female it does not construct that differentiation. Gender differentiation is promoted by/exacerbated through capitalist relations of production but is constructed elsewhere in the 'relatively autonomous' sphere of the family. This appreciation of the fact that an adequate understanding of the workings of capitalism cannot derive from the sphere of capitalist activity alone has reinforced the Althusserian view that not only are 'superstructural' elements of the social formation 'relatively auto-nomous' but that they contribute creatively to its overall structuring. This view of the economy as determinant 'in the last instance' but not necessarily structurally dominant thus rescued the analysis of ideology from the wilderness it occupied while the economy was assumed to be the source of all structural forms within capitalist society. This view of ideology as creative structurally is central to deciphering the reasons for the creation of 'disabilities' within capitalist society for they are created *within* the relatively auto-nomous sphere of the ideological.

Among the academic discourses on ideology and its expressive component 'culture' — that interaction between 'patterns learned and created in the mind and patterns communicated and made active in relationships, conventions and institutions' (Williams, 1965, p. 94) — the theories of ideological practice which have most constructive-ly dealt with the reproduction of structured inequalities have stressed the importance of the socio-cultural creation, manifestation and exploitation of *difference.* But here again, those who have begun to deal effectively with non-class-based inequalities, as we must, have been led by the inadequacy of existing theories of socio-cultural difference to look deeper. While theories such as that of Bourdieu (1977), concentrating on cultural difference, deal effectively with how society and culture work, with everyday cultural practice, particularly with regard to the reproduction of inequalities based in 'unconscious' categories such as class, deriving ultimately from the relations of production, they have done little to enlighten us about more direct forms of oppression, rooted in the psyche and the way we think — sexism, racism and discrimination in terms of disabili-ties. Even at the level of class-based inequalities we learn much about how they are reproduced through cultural difference, 'collec-tively orchestrated without being the product of the orchestrating action of a conductor' (p. 72) but little about how these differences are conceptualized. The deeper links with other forms of discrimina-tion are missing. Those links, which are vital to our theoretical project, are provided by Bisseret (1979).

In her search for the basic assumptions underlying the rationa-lization of school-based assessments, Bisseret reveals the central importance of an ideology of natural aptitudes in the educational systems of the West. She discusses 'the handicap which ties down members of specific social categories to specific aptitudes', pointing out that 'nothing can bridge the fundamental lack, which is presupposed and imposed' (p. 25). It is a way of thinking, a mode of thought which perceives 'others' as unitary and stable — defined once and for all in terms of their *natural* aptitudes. There is constant recourse to an 'essentialist ideology'.

Poststructural feminists — a plurality, a diversity, feminist discourses based in difference, for there is, contrary to Weedon's aspirations (1987, p. 20), no singular, unitary feminist poststructuralism — extend Bisseret's critique further as they explore the tyranny, the oppressiveness of the control of difference via language, the oppression/suppression/containment of diverse subjectivities. They explore the tyranny of male epistemic control as women are, to use Spivak's (1987) powerful phrases, *insidiously objectified,* the victims of an *epistemic violence.* So, for example, the deconstructionist projects of Gayatri Chakravorty Spivak (1987) her critiques of radical Indian historiography (the Subaltern Studies Group) in particular Chapter 12, reveal the way in which a mechanistic, phallogocentric mode of analysis distorts and subverts even the most admirable anti-capitalist or anti-imperialist academic projects. Most importantly, the need for discrete analytical categories and for some sort of generalized, unitary subject — the pupil, the working class, the subaltern — the reversion to an essentialist strategy, constantly subverts the subversive enterprise.

Spivak's awareness of these epistemic modes of oppression goes beyond Bourdieu's view of practice to reveal limits to strategic action which encompass those imposed by structurally-based variations in cultural capital, revealing the contours of symbolic violence and of forms of oppression which Bourdieu does not deal with — sexism and imperialism. Her analysis is relevant not only to sexist and imperialist forms of oppression — and for Spivak imperialist oppression is a mode of oppression which characterizes sexism — but as forcefully as ever to discrimination in terms of 'disability'. The domination of the 'disabled' is direct and all-encompassing. The reproduction of these inequalities occurs through the agency of the oppressors. The 'conductor' is present; the 'orchestration' overt. There is no sense in which the 'disabled' themselves construct a habitus for the next generation of 'disabled'. The disabled are the victims of an *epistemic violence,* coupled with overt physical control with no pretence of self-determination.

The unitary, phallogocentric mode of thought that marginalizes/belittles the 'female' in Western society does an even more complete job of segregating the 'disabled'. Only once essentialist ideology is understood as epistemic violence can the particular qualities of its effect on those defined 'disabled' be appreciated. First the ideology must be placed in historical perspective.

The Cosmological Tyranny of Science

The roots of this epistemic violence, its enabling cosmology, lie in the triumph of a mechanistic science over its spiritualist opponents in the fifteenth and sixteenth centuries, a triumph bemoaned by Blake and Goethe, explored at length in varied ways by Foucault and Derrida among others, and recently documented by Jit Singh Uberoi.

Let us turn first to Blake's *Jerusalem:*

> ... The Spectre, like a hoar-forest and a mildew, rose over Albion,
> Saying: 'I am God, O Sons of Men! I am your Rational Power!
> Am I not Bacon and Newton and Locke, who teach Humility to Man
> Who teach Doubt and Experiment? ...
> William Blake, Jerusalem (p. 398)

It is revealing to note that in her 'Dictionary of Proper Names' in *William Blake: The Complete Poems (1977)*, Ostriker writes:

> SPECTRE: The masculine principles which may divide from a being when his feminine portion ... separates, to assume independent life. Usually 'the reasoning power in man', *it is brutal, obsessive and selfish, and must be reintegrated.* (pp. 1054-5, emphasis added)

And again from *Jerusalem:*

> ... O Divine Spirit! sustain me on they wings,
> That I may awake Albion from his long and cold repose;
> For Bacon and Newton, sheath'd in dismal steel, their terrors hang
> Like iron scourges over Albion. Reasonings like vast Serpents
> Enfold around my limbs, bruising my minute articulations.
>
> I turn my eyes to the Schools and Universities of Europe
> And there behold the Loom of Locke, whose woof rages dire,
> Wash'd by the Water-wheels of Newton: black the cloth
> In heavy wreaths folds over every Nation: cruel Works

> Of many Wheels I view, wheel without wheel, with cogs tyrannic,
> Moving by compulsion each other, not as those in Eden, which,
> Wheel within wheel, in freedom revolve, in harmony and peace.
>
> William Blake, Jerusalem (p. 388)

The Eden referred to is a cosmos understood in terms of alternative 'sciences'. It is the 'nature' of Paracelsus, of Goethe, of Steiner which sees the individual not as a unitary subject but expressive of diverse qualities and rhythms in the natural world of sensitive chaos, of flux, not ordered and governed by laws but constantly forming and transforming, in chaos and in harmony. It is Cixous' Realm of the Gift. It is a world in stark contrast to the logocentric, unitary, law-governed ordered image that comes down to us in the science of Copernicus, Galileo and Newton. This Eden stands in contrast to what Goethe called the 'empirico-mechanico-dogmatic torture chamber' — scientific experts who cannot see nature, masked by the mode of thought, of perception, perpetuated as understanding.

We cannot pursue in detail the emergence and dominance of unitary, phallogocentric thought here, but it is essential to explore further the direct links between the victory of mechanistic science over its spiritualist opponent and the emergence of capitalism, for in the interplay of ideological and economic factors in the seventeenth century lie the seeds of discrimination on the basis of disabilities. Therein lies the birth of the clinic, of madness/sanity *and* of the segregation of 'the disabled'. The medical model that emerged with the clinic, the 'gaze' that defined/understood the patient, the dependence on the 'normal' to diagnose, to teach, to understand, created the disabled, depended on them to secure 'knowledge'.

The development of the mechanical model is associated with a particular view of nature — a 'sensible' view — accessible to the five senses. A nature governed by laws and viewed as a system, viewed mechanically as a union of parts, each part capable of being treated independently of the others — a jigsaw puzzle, tangible, measurable. An entity to be classified through the development of taxonomies. The laws could be deciphered and thenceforth *nature could be mastered,* controlled through the development of scientific *technology.* The techniques had but to be developed and learnt.

In contrast with the mechanical model, the 'holistic' or 'spiritual' models do not treat nature as a mechanical system but as dynamic, living, diverse. Nature is in sensitive balance, so too is the 'body'. The doctor must work in union with nature, not in opposition to or control of nature. So the old adage, oft-repeated by such alternative views of the science of medicine, 'nature heals, the doctor nurses'. For such a science, skill, empathy, art, intuition, sensitivity are fundamental to the effective exercising of the science, so the *art* of medicine. Neither techniques nor technology dominate. In medicine, the mechanical model comes down to us as orthodox modern medicine while the alternative view is to be found in alternative therapies such as homeopathy and anthroposophic medicine and in folk, essentially female, traditions. At a broad level the mechanical model is science, and the alternative model is non-science because it is deemed dependent on information beyond the objective, rational, sensible world of techniques and technology. Science claimed only one kind of explanation was valid, the rest were indulgence in the aesthetic and the mystical, even the satanic. So the Indian anthropologist/sociologist Jit Singh Uberoi (1984) writes of the great late eighteenth century and early nineteenth century German philosopher Goethe:

> Goethe as a scientist was dismissed in Europe as a poet, who had strayed beyond his proper place on the map of knowledge, and a dabbler. (p. 10)

Goethe, champion of Paracelsus, author of *Faust,* the work which explores the depths of his science, his view of the world, asserted:

> People forgot that science had developed from poetry, and they failed to take into consideration that a swing of the pendulum might beneficiently reunite the two, at a higher level and to mutual advantage. (quoted p. 19)

Integral to the emergence of mechanistic science with its stress on progress through knowledge, reason, rationality, was the Cartesian distinction between mind and body. The mind/body dualism, while elevating the products of the human mind to the status of eternal, disembodied knowledge, stressed the materiality of the body, to be understood like any other physical object. And so in the development of 'scientific' medicine. The clinical gaze was directed to the physical body understood from knowledge gained from cadavers, from a lifeless object:

> . . . the balance of experience required that the gaze directed upon the individual and the language of description should rest upon the stable, visible, legible basis of death. (p. 196)

The domain within which the discourse of medicine developed was 'that of a perpetual and objectively based correlation of the visible and the expressible' (p. 196). Thus did

> Western man ... constitute himself in his own eyes as an object of science, he grasped himself within his language, and gave himself, in himself and by himself, a discursive existence, only in the opening created by his own elimination: from the experience of Unreason was born psychology, the very possibility of psychology; from the integration of death into medical thought is born a medicine *that is given as a science of the individual.* (p. 197, emphasis added)

Medical science defined the individual as a physical entity, the sum of its parts, judged not on the basis of its dynamic, qualitative, health or sickness but in terms of its 'regularity', its 'normality', in terms of deviations from a physical 'norm'. This concentration on normality placed medical power in the hands of the specialist doctors, those with the clinical gaze, those who through their *'fine* sensibility' (p. 121) to the physical facts exercise 'the technical armature of the medical gaze ... "great sagacity", "great attention", "great precision", "great skill", "great patience" ' (p. 121).

> ... up to the end of the eighteenth century medicine related much more to health than to normality ... Nineteenth-century medicine, on the other hand, was regulated more in accordance with normality than with health; it formed its concepts and prescribed its interventions in relation to a standard of functioning and organic structure, and physiological knowledge — once marginal and purely theoretical knowledge for the doctor ... (p. 35)

So ideologically powerful did the medical model become, and with it the *male* doctors, that *it became, and they embodied, the mode in which one thought about humanity in general:*

> When one spoke of the life of groups and societies, of the life of the race, or even of the 'psychological life', one did not think first of the internal structure of *the organized being,* but of *the medical bipolarity of the normal and the pathological.* (p. 35)

How and why did the mechanical model triumph as orthodoxy?

The answer is essentially political and at base economic, rooted in the economic and political transformation of Britain and Europe in the fifteenth century. Europe was in turmoil.

The loose federation of Christendom broke down and new nationalisms began to assert themselves. The authority of both church and nobility was questioned. It was an era of uprisings. The black death of the fourteenth century had devastated the population, radically affecting the supply of labour, and generating changes in labour relations. A dissatisfied and drastically reduced labour force in the towns was ruthlessly oppressed with wage controls and the assertion of feudal obligations while the ruling class sought to expand its increasingly urban-oriented life-style through trade and plunder. Wage relations replaced reciprocal (though unequal) feudal ties. 'Knight service increasingly gave way to mercenary captains and paid violence. The civil population were everywhere the victims' (Anderson, 1974, p. 201). Church rebelled against church, the state rebelled against the church; and the peasantry rebelled against the church and state.

As economics and politics were in turmoil so too was the field of knowledge. A new human-centred intellectual tradition emerged which saw human intellectual activity as the source of knowledge. So philosophy moved more and more into a secular arena, as virulent a battlefield as that on which the peasants fought. Why and how then did one sort of science triumph? *Essentially because it served the economy and the polity well.* From the beginning of the battle between mechanistic science and the non-mechanistic sciences it was the non-mechanistic sciences which were radical, which rebelled against the establishment, for example the wandering magus Paracelsus. He was brilliant, way ahead of his time in his understanding of medicine in particular, especially in the use of chemically-based medicines.

As far as many of his contemporaries were concerned he worked miracles but he never claimed to do more than help nature to work effectively. He rebelled against the academic conventions of his time, pampering to no-one, criticising his contemporaries, constantly rocking the boat and being denounced by the establishment. He supported the peasants in their struggles and asserted that science must be for the people and of the people. 'Convinced that science must learn from the people and work for the people, he wrote in the vernacular' (p. 200).

But the mechanistic model triumphed. To quote Jit Singh Uberoi (1984) again:

> The victory of official modernity in the scientific revolution
> of the mid-seventeenth century, which ran parallel to the

restoration of the monarchy over the ruins of the Puritan revolution in England (1660), is to be dated with apparent finality from the battle of Kepler the continental against the science and the philosophy of Fludd, the last Paracelsian in England (1621, etc.). The Copernican tradition then became dominant and official, and the Paracelsian tradition became recessive and went underground for the future. Elements of the latter remained secretly active in Europe, however, viewing the so-called Copernican revolution as essentially a counter-revolution according to their radical faith. If the world-view of Copernicus, Galileo and Newton came to be embodied in the recovered myth of Prometheus, the official hero of European modernity and the benefactor of mankind who defiantly stole fire from Olympus and suffered the vengeance of the gods, then the Paracelsian world-view also came to be embodied in the more popular myth of Faust, the anti-hero of the underground who sold his soul to the devil in exchange for knowledge and power in his own lifetime. The reciprocal dialogue, or perhaps the lack of it, between the world of Prometheus and the world of Faust gives us the key to assess the full measure of modernity in science, religion and politics in Europe. (p. 21)

The establishment of the science of Copernicus, Galileo and Newton as the *official* scientific method was overtly political, associated for example with the founding of the Royal Society of London, founded after the restoration of the monarchy in 1660. 'Truth' did not win out. Nor did the new supercede the old.

To quote Redner (1987):

> ... this new scientific authority structure incorporated by Royal edict was closely related to as well as dependent on the political authority of the newly arisen absolutist monarchies. ... the authority of the cognitive norms of the new Mechanical Philosophy was itself protected by royal power from the challenges of politically more dangerous approaches to science then current: for example, those deriving from such Baconian reformists as Comenius, and from Paracelsian iatrochemists and hermeticists like Fludd ... a 'harmless' and politically innocuous scientific approach was instituted at the expense of more dangerous radical rivals, which were thereby suppressed and repressed into irrational currents of popular science and the occult. (pp. 44-5)

Science thus meant 'the mechanical model' and was oriented towards technological supremacy as a means to the effective *control* of nature *and of humanity*. But science soon penetrated everyday life as the scientific experts became the 'theologians' serving the interests of those in positions of economic and political power. Glorification of God was displaced by a glorification of the *scientific method* — rational, and ordered, the product of human minds but beyond any individual mind — a logical procedure free of individual vagaries. Faith in God gives way to a faith in science, a faith in the reproduction of rational knowledge and advancement towards the rational society. Prejudices are then legitimized by scientific rather than religious experts who, no less than the clergy of the past, retreat from responsibility for the way their theories are used, to the monasteries of today's 'theologians', the universities.

With orthodox science firmly set in its mechanistic mode the scene had been set for the intellectual euphoria of the so-called Enlightenment. 'Progress' was now assured through science, 'an autonomous human creation, not the expression of the divine purpose working itself out on earth' (Kumar, 1978, p. 22).

> The future beckoned urgently, and the promise it held out could only adequately be gauged by the chaos that might result if the forces of progress were not all combined in the task of bringing the new society into being. Of those forces the most important were science, the men of science, and all those who could see in the achievements of the scientific method the highest fulfilment of the Enlightenment, and the key to the future direction and organization of society. (p. 26)

But it was a progress grounded in capitalist production, in relations of production which demanded easily hired and easily fired, uniform, dependable, *able-bodied* labour power, factory fodder, 'variable capital'. In the field of medicine in particular, the human individual was being redefined in such a way as to ensure an ideological practice which served the labour market, and the egos of the wealthy, well. The medical model, through the birth of the clinic and the asylum, established the contours of humanity, of *normality,* which the economy and the polity required. These new contours of humanity created the 'disabled'.

The link between the creation of 'disabilities' and capitalism is complex to say the least. It would be pushing even vulgar materialism a long way to claim that the emergence of the 'disabled' is the result of the need of capitalism for an underclass of disabled workers. But there is a vital link. Their marginalization is an essential part of capitalist ideology. They are the 'other' against which arbitrary 'normality' is maintained. The practices directed towards those that the medical gaze judges 'disabled' exemplify the ideological core of our society, the central mode of thought. Without them the whole ideological edifice collapses. For capitalist production is grounded in a basic ideological dependence on a perception of each person as unitary, contained by and identified as their physical body, bounded in time by birth (or possibly conception) and death, equal with others *before the law,* individuated legally, politically, economically (labour relations, property rights) and spiritually (privatized religious adherence).

The historical foundations of concepts of 'the disabled', 'the handicapped', 'the sub-normal', 'the mentally retarded', lie, therefore, not in the mechanization of labour processes in the eighteenth century, in the transformation of the relations of production, but in the triumph of a politically innocuous mechanistic, unitary science over its more spiritualist, non-unitary and radical opponents in the sixteenth century, in the transformation of cosmology. Royal patronage of the new mechanistic science set the scene for the development of industrial capitalism out of the ruins of feudalism and along the way imbued nature and humanity with taxonomies which capitalism could feed off but which it did not create — at one point looking to child and female labour, then rejecting them in favour of men, to return to them yet again along with ethnically distinct minorities once the male labour movement created the need for a new supply of cheap labour. Are the handicapped its next target, the newest underclass? *And is integration the unwitting agent in that process?*

This question must be at the back of our minds at all times for the influence of the mode of production 'in the last instance' is very powerful. Certainly the tyranny of this all-encompassing essentialist ideology, this unitary mode of thought, deeply grounded in the discursive constitution of the body, is most apparent in the lives of the disabled as their disabilities are created through constant testing, constant assessment, measured against pre-determined unitary models of retardation, aptitude and intelligence. Once they are assessed as abnormal, those models, syndromes, are the basis for prediction of the future by 'knowledgeable specialists'. The same obsession with 'intelligence' which is basic to ethnic/ideology of competition, which rationalises the vast inequalities of reward within the economy, which '. . . becomes the *scientific* warrant of a social organization which it justifies' (Bisseret, 1979, p. 20, emphasis added), marginalizes, institutionalizes the disabled.

Aptitude, intelligence, is assumed 'natural', a biological given, the basis of our 'order', 'discovered' (or rather imposed, predetermined by standardization to the 'normal curve') through class/sex/race/ability-biased testing processes, a 'natural order', an hierarchical order, a justifiable social inequality. When people score poorly in aptitude tests for cultural reasons — oppressed racial/ethnic groups, the working classes — they are assumed to be *lacking* in 'natural aptitude', 'defined by a lack' (p. 19). The lack of those who cannot respond because of physical or perceptual disabilities does not, as with the culturally deprived, simply rule them out of consideration for highly valued and lucrative employment, *'but defines them, condemns them, out of society itself.* They are not merely defined as low in the "natural order" but as positively *unnatural,* as outside the range of "natural" "normality" ' (Branson, Miller, Branson, 1988, p. 117) condemned beyond the margins of society and culture.

This 'scientific' evaluation by specialists extends to the society at large through their faith in the religion of science and its high priests. The disabled, the outcasts of this religion, its Untouchables, are condemned by its priesthood and shunned, even feared for their 'unnaturalness', by its congregation. 'Out of sight and out of mind they move in the shadows, on the margins of society's consciousness, *a living negativity, serving, by their very existence as a "negative" segregated group, to define the positive standards of "normality", "acceptability".'* (p. 117)

The Differences between Discrimination against the Disabled and Other Forms of Discrimination

While the battles to understand and destroy discrimination through the construction of disabilities have much to learn from feminist theory and politics, the particular nature of the epistemic, physical and psychological violence wreaked upon the disabled must not thereby be lost. As mentioned above, our essentialist ideology, an obsession with 'normality', defines/condemns the disabled *out of society, out of nature/humanity.* This is not the case with sexism. The nature of the *relationship* between the powerful and the powerless is fundamentally different.

Feminization is devaluation. Defined in phallogocentric terms, the feminine is deemed the inferior side of a relationship. The 'male' encompasses (cf Dumont, 1972) the 'female', determining its form, dependent on the 'female' as defined by the 'male', the 'masculine' constantly played off against the 'feminine' in relationships. 'Feminine' is a dynamic, albeit subordinate and unitary, subjectivity. So dominant is the 'feminine' as an image of compliance and inferiority, so all-encompassing is sexism, that some theorists have posited the constant metaphoric 'feminization' of oppressed groups other than women, to describe the quality of their relationship with the dominant group/elements in society; for example, the feminization of 'the masses' (e.g. Huyssen (1986), and Probyn's (1987) critique of Huyssen and discussion of associated issues).

But the 'disabled' are not feminized. They are denied a relationship with their oppressors, a place in society *and culture*. In the discursive constitution of the body in capitalist society, sexuality is central (Foucault, 1981). In the discursive constitution of the 'normal' body (see Foucault 1975) the 'disabled' are discarded, their 'normality' and thus their sexuality denied. They are desexed, degendered and thus dehumanized. Their oppression does not involve 'boundary maintenance' within social life as is the case with sexism or racism, nor does it involve ongoing strategies of exclusion to ensure the ongoing dominance of the oppressors. The 'disabled' offer no immediate, tangible gratification, nothing that the 'able-bodied' *want* — no pleasure, no labour. The 'disabled' threaten with their presence. *They are an ideological necessity in a humanist world based in 'normality'.* Their existence is of central importance for their asocial presence — they are 'there' reinforcing the social, cultural 'normality' of others — maintains the illusion of the reality of nature viewed mechanistically as ordered, bounded, tangible, humanity integrated through the physically-based clinical gaze. *They define the limits of humanity* and even when rarely integrated (except in exceptional circumstances in environments governed by alternative cosmologies such as the Anthroposophists, the followers of the teachings of the Goethian scientist/philosopher Rudolf Steiner (see Branson, Miller and Branson, 1988)), do so as an abnormal presence. All 'disabled' are 'touched' by this treatment of the 'severely disabled'. They are all seen as at least vaguely inhuman. They all threaten with their presence, the embodiment of something beyond understanding, beyond the bounds of the 'sensible'/'cultural' world, something 'supernatural'. To define is to control but to define is to deny/turn away from the realities of difference beyond the artificial bounds of definition. To define is to establish contradictions which one can turn one's back on but never escape. So the 'female' uncontained is deemed a witch, the 'disabled' uncontained, an ogre, a living gargoyle. In the assertion of difference lies liberation. Feminist politics provides clues here too, but first what of 'integration'?

Integration: Policy, Programme, Ideology

Integration as concept and policy tends toward the stabilization of the categories it seeks to destroy for it is constructed in the same mode as its segregationist opposite — the familiar comfort of a unitary world in which appearances become accepted fact, reformists effectively supporting the tyranny they oppose through their very opposition to it. Normality can only be achieved through its destruction, not by the integration of the 'normal' and 'abnormal'.

In this sense *integration must be a policy, a programme, oriented towards its own destruction,* aiming to destroy the very categories which are seen as needing to be 'integrated' into the 'normal' world. If the disabled are 'normal', so much an accepted part of our world that we take their presence, their humanity, their special qualities for granted, then there can be no 'integration' for there is no 'segregation', either *conceptually,* in terms of categories, taxonomies, or *actually,* in terms of institutional separation.

And this is the crunch. The unwitting complicity of the integrationist is the same as the unwitting complicity of the committed academic. Unable to transcend what Bisseret calls 'essentialist ideology', to understand their research and writing within the context of the discourse of their culture and transcend it, as Foucault did in his own rejection of his archaeological method (see Dreyfus and Rabinow, 1982) they are incapable of understanding that imperialist mode of oppression which robs those it oppresses of their subjectivity, of their strategic, creative agency. Writing of the radical intellectual in the West who approaches the oppressed as a unitary subject, Spivak (1987) writes:

> Although some of these Western intellectuals express genuine concern about the ravages of contemporary neo-colonialism in their own nation-states, they are not knowledgeable in the history of imperialism, in *the epistemic violence* that constituted/effaced a subject that was obliged to cathect (occupy in response to a desire) the space of the Imperialists' self-consolidating other. (p. 209)

What is required, she says, is the epistemological self-consciousness of a deconstructionist approach:

> A deconstructive approach would bring into focus the fact that they are themselves engaged in an attempt at displacing discursive fields, that they themselves 'fail' (in the general sense) for reasons as 'historical' as those they adduce for the heterogeneous agents they study; and would attempt to forge a practice that would take this into acount. Otherwise, refusing to acknowledge the implications of their own line of work because that would be politically incorrect, they would, willy-nilly, 'insidiously objectify' the subaltern, *control him through knowledge even as they restore versions of causality and self-determination to him, become complicit, in their desire for totality* (and therefore totalization), with a 'law [that] assign[s] a[n] undifferentiated [proper] name' to 'the subaltern as such'. (p. 201, emphasis added)

So does integration, as an ideology, as a practice, control the disabled, 'insidiously objectify' through dependence on a unitary subject within a totally-conceived, easily administered, manageable, comfortable-to-think-about order.

In orienting integration towards its own destruction we work constantly against the grain, against our inclinations, against comfort, against our common sense, our humanism, against logic, against epistemology, against science — against our habitus, our structured dispositions, our structuring structures. Our colonial mentality would mould others to our ways. We have grown unaccustomed over centuries to acknowledging/respecting other modes of thought, other possible truths. We administer everything — humanity, nature. We yearn for *coherent policy* — the key to effective administration. We yearn for rules. We assume that they will be obeyed or disobeyed — law and order, phallogocentrism — the phallic weapon/unifier/order/centre/linchpin — 'reason'. Other possibilities are excluded. Our *perception* is of a normal world — the disabled the victims of our perceptions, our assumptions as to how things are.

But practice is not lawful; meaning is constantly deferred; unity an illusion. We exclude the disabled and then depend for effective practice on evading normality, on breaking rules. Reviewing Kathy Acker's *The Empire of the Senseless*, Boyd Tonkin (1988) writes:

> *Empire of the Senseless* signs off with a startlingly funny

sequence in which Abhor on a motorbike plays havoc with the traffic when she tries to adhere to the Highway Code. That semanticist's test-case of a rule-governed system leads straight to chaos and confusion. 'Disobeying rules is the same as following rules', she concludes, 'cause it's necessary to listen to your own heart'? (p. 31).

But for us to be able to break them they must be asserted. *For us to scorn normality, the ordinary, the abnormal must be embodied.* We are strategists, and rules, normality, are essential to our strategies. For us to be strategists, agents of the reproduction of our society and culture, consciously and unconsciously, we wreak epistemic violence on the disabled and in the process *exclude them from strategy.* The scandalous behaviour of the British Nabobs in India rested on assertions of law, order, civilization, on the definition of the colonized as a unitary other, as negative, as in need of law, order, civilization, while never capable of attaining them. It rested, depended, on this epistemic violence, on this destruction of their varied, multifaceted, constantly transforming vitalities.

So we destroy the disabled. So we provide therapy as a denial of the possibility of the attainment of humanity. Integrate them as disabled. Integration as a policy is so easy to think about, enthuse about, more of the same with a twist, a spicy twist, a twist that is so easily no more than strategic fashion, for the disabled remain. That is, unless we see the contradictions and read against the grain of the policy, the programme, of conventional criticism, subversion; against the grain of conservatism and radicalism alike; against the grain of our own critique, our own culture. Only then do we begin to understand what we do to others and ourselves. But most of all what we do to those we render powerless, to those we homogenize, outcast in the service of our egos, the disabled.

Where to go? The clues lie beyond and through our culture to other cultures not defined as other, to relationships beyond individualism, to medicine beyond the medical model; beyond models, in the assertion of difference, in the denial of normality, to seek to understand, rather than to fear, mystery. We must listen to those modes of expression less contained by logocentrism, the legitimate descendants of spiritualist science — poetry, drama, painting, song . . .

Death of Son (Who died in a mental hospital aged one)

Something has ceased to come along with me.

Something like a person: something very like one.
    And there was no nobility in it
        Or anything like that.

Something was there like a one year
Old house, dumb as stone. While the near buildings
    Sang like birds and laughed
        Understanding the pact

They were to have with silence. But he
Neither sang nor laughed. He did not bless silence
    Like bread, with words.
        He did not forsake silence.

But rather, like a house in mourning
Kept the eye turned to watch the silence while
    The other houses like birds
        Sang around him.

And the breathing silence neither
Moved nor was still.

I have seen stones: I have seen brick
But this house was made up of neither bricks nor stone
    But a house of flesh and blood
        With flesh of stone

And bricks for blood. A house
Of stones and blood in breathing silence with the other
    Birds singing crazy on its chimneys.
        But this was silence.

This was something else, this was
Hearing and speaking though he was a house drawn
    Into silence, this was
        Something religious in his silence.

Something shining in his quiet,
This was different this was altogether something else:
    Though he never spoke, this
        Was something to do with death.

And then slowly the eyes stopped looking
Inward. The silence rose and became still.
The look turned to the out place and stopped,
    With the birds still shrilling around him.
        And as if he could speak

He turned over on his side with his one year
Red as a wound
He turned over as if he could be sorry for this
And out of his eyes two great tears rolled, like stones, and he
died.

Jon Silkin, 1980, pp. 8-9

Just as Iragaray (1985) explores the 'otherness' of female sexuality, 'this sex which is not one', the repressed aspects of being a woman, we must explore the 'otherness' of the 'disabled'. This is not to deny the pain, the frustration, the confusion, the heartache of physical and perceptual difficulties but rather to stress the creativity of difference, the infinite variability of subjectivity, the subtlety and richness of sensibilities and sensitivities beyond those allowed by logocentric 'common sense', or mechanistic 'science'.

Poststructuralism provides the stimulus therefore not only to undermine a phallogocentric mode of thought that insidiously objectifies but to assert, like much feminism does for women, the special, hidden, repressed, creative qualities of 'the disabled'. In a society moulded in terms of a myopic, claustrophobic logocentrism, encompassed by and glorifying a unitary, intensely physical version of 'maleness' — Blake's 'Spectre': brutal, obsessive, selfish — we must turn to the 'other' for enlightenment, to the 'female', the colonised, the 'disabled'.

That is the way we must think. That is the way we must dispose ourselves towards others, define ourselves in relation to others. We are strategists engaging in ideological practice. We must *act,* as well as read, against the grain, make manifest the contradictions in behaviour. We must, like Lou Brown in Madison, Wisconsin face people with the 'other' but not *as* the 'other'. People must not be allowed to 'turn their backs'. Our policies/programmes must defy the logics of bureaucracy just as our academic criticisms of them must not be logocentric. If we criticize in terms of an essentialist ideology we subvert our own subversive intent. We may thereby succeed in generating programmes which improve the lot of 'the disabled' but we do not face the real challenge to destroy the view of humanity and its ideological practice which marks them off as a unitary 'other' in the first place.

One reaction to this chapter may be — 'lots of high faluting words, lots of academic jargon, airy-fairy playing with words, but what about reality? What do we do? How do we cope with those who cannot care for themselves (have we created their dependence?), with incontinence, lack of motor coordination, inabilities to com-

165

municate (in conventional terms)?' That is the crux of the problem. We insist on being *practical,* on finding *practical solutions* in a neat and tidy administrative framework. And so you/we subordinate the needs of those to *your/our* need for a *'reasonable', 'coherent'* framework for action. Our logocentrism, our *dependence* on essentialist ideology is as addictive as any drug of dependence. Our society is hooked on a way of thinking, a way of acting. To change is to suffer painful withdrawal symptoms, disorientation, but if the 'disabled' are to return to the world we must change.

The critique of policy cannot be done from within the framework that the policy has been written in the first place. We must stand back from policy to see its shortcomings. We cannot expect to solve problems within existing structures of thought and practice.

References

ABBERLEY, P. (1987) 'The Conception of Oppression and the Development of a Social Theory of Disability' in *Disability, Handicap and Society,* 2, 1, pp. 5-20.

ANDERSON, P. (1974) *Passages from Antiquity to Feudalism,* London, New Left Books.

BARRETT, M. (1980) *Women's Problems Today: Problems in Marxist Feminist Analysis,* London, Verso.

BISSERET, N. (1979) *Education, Class Language and Ideology,* London, Routledge and Kegan Paul.

BLAKE, W. (1934) *The Poetical Works of William Blake,* London, Oxford University Press.

BOURDIEU, P. (1977) *Outline of a Theory of Practice,* London, Cambridge University Press.

BOURDIEU, P. and PASSERON, C. (1970) *Reproduction in Education, Society and Culture,* New York, Sage.

BRANSON, J. and MILLER, D. (1977) 'Feminism and Class Struggle' in *Arena,* 47-48, pp. 80-97.

BRANSON, J., MILLER, D. and BRANSON, K. (1988) An Obstacle Race: A Case Study of a Child's Schooling in Australia and England in *Disability, Handicap and Society,* 3, 2.

CIXOUS, H. and CLEMENT, C. (1987) 'The Newly Born Women' (trans. B. WING) in *Theory and History of Literature,* 24, Minneapolis, Minnesota University Press.

DREYFUS, H.L. and RABINOW, P. (1982) *Michel Foucault: Beyond Structuralism and Hermeneutics,* Brighton, Harvester Press.

DUMONT, L. (1980) *Homo Hierarchies,* Chicago, Chicago University Press.

ECO, U. (1984) *The Name of the Rose,* London, Picador.

FOUCAULT, M. (1975) *The Birth of the Clinic,* New York, Vintage Books.

FOUCAULT, M. (1981) *The History of Sexuality,* Volume I, Harmondsworth, Penguin.

HALL, D.G.E. (1968) *History of South East Asia,* London, Macmillan.

HUYSSEN, A. (1986) 'Mass Culture as Woman: Modernisms Other' in MODLESKI, T. (Ed.) *Studies in Entertainment: Critical Approaches to Mass Culture,* Bloomington and Indianapolis, Indiana University Press, pp. 188-208.

IRAGARAY, L. (1985) *Speculum of the Other Woman* (translated by Gillian C. GILL), Ithaca, New York, Cornell University Press.

KUMAR, K. (1978) *Prophecy and Progress,* Harmondsworth, Penguin.

MILLER, D. and BRANSON, J. (1987) 'Pierre Bourdieu: Culture and Praxis' in AUSTIN-BROOS, D. (Ed.), *Creating Culture,* Sydney, Allen and Unwin.

MOI, T. (1985) *Sexual Textual Politics,* London, Methuen.

MOI, T. (Ed.) (1986) *The Kristeva Reader,* London, Polity Press.

OSTRIKER, A. (Ed.) (1977) *William Blake: The Complete Poems,* London, Penguin.

PROBYN, E. (1987) 'Bodies and Anti-Bodies: Feminism and the Post Modern' in *Cultural Studies,* 1, 3, pp. 349ff.

REDNER, H. (1987) 'The Institutionalization of Science: A Critical Synthesis' in *Social Epistemology,* 1, pp. 37-59.

SILKIN, J. (1980) *Selected Poems,* London, Routledge and Kegan Paul.

SPIVAK, G.C. (1987) *In Other Worlds: Essays in Cultural Politics,* London, Methuen.

STRATHERN, M. (1985) 'Dislodging a World View: Challenge and Counter-Challenge in the Relationship between Feminism and Anthropology' in *Australian Feminist Studies,* 1, pp. 1-15.

TONKIN, B. (1988) 'Acts of Profane Rebellion' in *New Statesman,* 13 May.

UBEROI, J.S. (1978) *Science and Culture,* New Delhi, Oxford University Press.

UBEROI, J.S. (1984) *The Other Mind of Europe,* New Delhi, Oxford University Press.

WEEDON, C. (1987) *Feminist Practice and Poststructural Theory,* Oxford, Basil Blackwell.

WILLIAMS, R. (1965) *The Long Revolution,* Harmondsworth, Penguin.

Chapter 9

Working Report: Educating Children and Young People with Disabilities or Difficulties in Learning in The People's Republic of China

---

Patricia Potts

Introduction

'Special Education for the Disabled in China' was the title of a news item in *Spare Rib,* January 1987. The information had come from the December 1986 issue of *Women of China,* an English-language magazine produced by the All China Women's Federation. This magazine described how the rights of people with disabilities were being discussed and how special educational provision was developing to reflect a new commitment. I decided to aim for a trip to China during my study leave, due in a year's time. Around March, 1987, I received advance notice of a conference on special education to be held in Beijing in June, 1988, so I sent off an abstract and learned in the autumn that it had been accepted.

I spent three weeks in China and visited, amongst other places, eight special schools: two schools for 'mentally retarded' children, two for deaf children and young people, two for blind children and young people and one 'correctional' school. I also visited one mental health institution and one kindergarten.

In Britain we stress independence, individuality and personal development. Would this be true in a society where views of the self and the value given to independence are very different? I found that the issues of conformity versus diversity and self-help versus community support are just as central in China as they are in the West but are debated within a context of quite different traditions, values and aspirations.

I have come to understand difficulties in learning as a mismatch between pupils' interests and abilities and the curricula and support they are offered. The nature of any mismatch will, of course, vary according to the context. For example, the problems faced by young children in China learning to read and write characters may be unlike those of English-speaking children learning to combine phonic rules and sight recognition in order to read an alphabetic language. The tasks are very different. Teaching and learning relationships are bound by separate cultural traditions.

The Context of Special Education in The People's Republic of China.

Traditionally, attitudes towards people with disabilities in China have been negative, for a variety of reasons. These include the economic hardship that often followed from having a disabled person in the family, the custom that your sons would look after you in your old age, the intolerance of differences in appearance and behaviour, and the more recent pressure to conform to ideal types, such as 'model worker' or 'model teacher'. People with disabilities were un-ideal types.

During the 1980s the one-child policy has been adhered to, particularly in the cities. Although many people agree with this attempt to control the population, the effect has been to highlight parents' desire for a healthy son, thus discriminating against both girls and children with disabilities. The concession that allows you to have a second child if your first is born with a disability colludes with this desire.

Parent-child relationships are rapidly changing in China and children are under great pressure to excel. Schools for parents, themselves mostly young and whose own education was interrupted by the cultural revolution, are being set up to cope with these stresses.

Life in China is organized on an institutional basis: family, school, workplace. There is no national social security system or network of personal social services. There are very few mobility aids, and welfare benefits are distributed from the school or workplace. If you are not in school or you are unable to work, then you remain with your family, which does not receive any specific support, or you live in a social welfare institution run by your local Bureau of Civil Affairs.

There are therefore no area-based or interdisciplinary services: no social workers, speech therapists, health visitors or educational psychologists. The people who are involved with the identification and referral to special educational provisions of children with disabilities or learning difficulties are parents, class teachers, doctors and administrators.

The only slogan I came across when I was in China was 'One country, two systems', which refers to the opening up of economic activity prior to the return of Hong Kong to China in 1997. There is some decentralization of control over private enterprises. This may mean that services for people with disabilities will develop in addition to those run by the state. Existing examples include the Hong Kong charitable funding for the special school in Guangzhou (see below) and World Health Organisation and UNICEF support for some of the provisions in Beijing.

Education

The aims of education for all young people in China are: the strengthening of socialism, the achievement of universal school attendance and literacy, and good health. There is no clear separation of education from work, and factories and schools are closely linked. At the entrance to the correctional school I visited, a decorative mural exhorted us to 'Face the world, face the future and face modernization'.

The mainstream education system is highly competitive in China as provisions, especially at the level of higher education, are scarce. Only about 4 per cent of middle (secondary) school leavers have the opportunity to go on to a college of some kind. Opportunities are noticeably greater in the cities than in the rural areas. There is a National Curriculum and pupils have to pass examinations to move up from stage to stage. The same books are used right across the country, in both ordinary and special schools. Classes are very large in ordinary schools — forty to fifty is common — and there is no mixed ability teaching. There is little group work or discussion in Chinese classrooms. Music and physical exercise are far more important to the Chinese than they are to educators in Britain.

The status of teachers is low in China and working conditions appear to be poor. Wages are lower than for factory workers. Unmarried teachers will probably share a dormitory room with two or three others, and they are usually assigned to their careers and have little say in what job they do. It is hard to change jobs or to change direction through inservice education. The legacy of the cultural revolution puts teachers in a difficult position, for education is stressed as being extremely important to the modernization of China but teachers themselves are not seen as being of the same value as factory workers. There were regular articles in the English-language *China Daily* about the possible restructuring of wages to give teachers and other professionals greater rewards. These reforms now seem to be in jeopardy (Mirsky, 1988)

China's pattern of international relations and the discontinuity of academic study as a result of the cultural revolution have both influenced the development of educational planning and research. People in senior posts in education authorities and universities will probably have read their psychology, for example, in Moscow in the fifties. Then, from the mid-sixties to the late seventies, psychology was a 'closed' subject, the bourgeois Western variety being criticized particularly for its personality theories (see Brown, 1981). Since 1979 it has once again been possible to read foreign journals and to go to the West to study. There is a special education section of the Beijing Educational Research Institute and there is a National Special Education Research Association, with local associations in the main cities. Special education research is new and is nothing like the boom industry it has become in the West.

Policy-making and Change

In May 1985, the Central Committee of the Communist Party of China held a national education conference. As a result, a Central Document was published containing the decision to reform the structure of education across the country. This Document is discussed in an article by Cheng Kai Ming in *Comparative Education* (Cheng, 1986).

In April, 1986, the Fourth Session of the Sixth National People's Congress adopted a new Law on Compulsory Education. Article 9 says:

> Local people's governments 'shall establish special schools (or classes) for children and adolescents who are blind, deaf-mute or retarded. The state encourages enterprises, establishments and other sectors to establish schools of the types prescribed by this law.'

The Law itself is brief, with 18 Articles in all. Article 17 says:

Detailed rules and regulations for the implementation of this law shall be drawn up by the department in charge of education under the State Council and shall come into force after approval by the State Council.

The standing committees of the people's congresses of provinces, autonomous regions and municipalities directly under the Central Government may, in the light of their local conditions, work out their own specific measures for implementing this law.

Voluntary activity is also increasing in China and the most influential figure here is the son of Deng Xiaoping, Deng Pufang. In 1984 he founded the China Welfare Fund for Handicapped People and he plays a crucial role in the development of services for people with disabilities or learning difficulties. He was thrown out of a high window by Red Guards in 1968 when he was a final-year student at one of Beijing's universities and his back was broken. He was the only person I saw in China using a wheelchair. Deng Pufang speaks tirelessly about the need for public attitudes to change and for adequate and appropriate educational services. In a newspaper interview he described what he calls 'humanitarian education'. He is aware of the delicacy of such a concept. 'Humanitarianism' belongs to the capitalist West and was invented by capitalist philanthropists. It also involves the consideration of people as individuals and a language of social participation that does not fit with the rhetoric of ideal types which is the basis of much of China's moral education (Liaowiang, 1985). Deng Pufang is actively concerned with the development of special education policy and gave the main address at the opening ceremony of the Beijing Special Education conference.

I encountered a number of tensions and contradictions when discussing education in China. For example, competitive excellence and equality of rights and opportunity are both stressed; 'handicap' is seen both as something fixed and as something that can be changed, and medical rehabilitation and the reduction of prejudice are often the joint themes of articles and speeches. More generally, people are encouraged both to see their group membership as a priority and to aspire to the example of exceptional heroes and heroines.

Chinese Views of Disability and Special Education

A medical approach to understanding children's disabilities and educational difficulties is common, with frequent references to brain-damage, heredity and abnormal birth experiences. A special educational curriculum derived from this approach would therefore be based on a typology of the characteristics associated with a particular disability and such a curriculum can be found in Chinese special schools. However, all schools also see responding to the needs of society as a priority. As special education is seen as part of the rehabilitation of people with disabilities, there is a clear focus on vocational training and compensating for deficits. A particularly instrumental view of education also follows from the fact that employment is socially as well as economically vital in China.

There is a good deal of self-criticism, though, and an openness to ideas and practices from abroad. For example, I often heard it acknowledged that there were far too many children not in any form of education, that negative attitudes towards people with disabilities do persist and that identification and referral procedures were unsystematic. I also heard expressed views which did reflect an awareness of the relevance of the social context of children's experiences and a desire to break down the stereotyped images of people with disabilities. One conference participant wrote in his abstract that we should aim to 'tap the intelligence of handicapped children' and another said that 'handicapped children have a lot in common with non-handicapped children'.

Among the developments called for by the Chinese at the moment are: appropriate technological aids and equipment, identification and assessment strategies for children with difficulties in learning or emotional problems, more support for parents and the encouragement of voluntary initiatives. As yet, the perspectives of children, young people and their parents have attracted little official attention. One mother of a teenage boy describes her feelings in this way:

> We didn't dare have a second child. What if we had another one like him? Perhaps we are being too sensitive but we do feel under pressure. We can't look the world in the face.

> We haven't had a happy day since . . . but you do get used to it, gradually. If you had a deaf-mute, for example, or a child with only one leg, the tongues wouldn't wag. But if you have a kid who's not too bright in the head then a lot of people will go on and on about you.

> I'd give my life to make him normal, I would. You don't
> know how much we love him and how terrible the pressure
> is.   (Zhang & Sang, 1986).

Changing District Special School for 'Mentally Retarded' Children, Shanghai

Shanghai has twelve inner city districts, ten outer districts and
thirteen million people. Each district has its school for deaf children,
but this is the only school specially for children whom we should
officially describe as having 'moderate learning difficulties'. In 1979,
a class was set up in the nearby school for deaf children, the first in
the country. The initiative was taken by Yin Chun Ming, my host
while I was in Shanghai, who was then deputy head of the Deaf
School and is now Shanghai's Inspector of Special Education.

There are ten or so pupils in each class, aged between 7 and 16.
They are referred from ordinary schools or nurseries or by their
families. A report is prepared by a university-based psychologist.
Pupils follow the National Curriculum but at a slower pace. I saw
children in the third grade doing first grade language work. Children
are discouraged from using their left hand in school in China except
for holding chopsticks at mealtimes.

The school building is six years old, a concrete oblong three
stories high. The desks are shiny light brown, descended from the
traditional lacquered finish. The classrooms are fairly small, with
rows of separate desks and a blackboard at each end, one for the
teacher and one for the pupils. There is a sewing room, for boys and
girls, a library, a large outside area for exercising and sport and a tiny
playground between the school and the flats at the back. We sat and
talked in a meeting room and had tea and Chinese Coke.

For about ninety pupils there are twenty-nine teachers and
helpers. The language teachers are the closest equivalent to our class
teachers and there were also teachers for craft, music, maths and
sport. The teachers have their own workroom. Yin Chun Ming
provides inservice education for the teachers; they have not
undergone specialist initial training. Training for special education
has begun in the last four years in Nanking and Beijing.

The teachers I met had been at the school for a long time. When
I showed the headteacher, Zhang Long, an article from the
International Child Welfare Review for 1979 about the setting up of the
new class she immediately recognized the boy in the accompanying

photograph (Shih, 1979). Another teacher later told me that he now has a job. At the moment, all the school's leavers get some kind of work.

There are no printed materials adapted for children with difficulties in learning because this is not seen as economically viable and few teachers have any means of reproducing materials they prepare themselves. They have to rely on the textbooks of the National Curriculum and their own handiwork. Supplies of paper for teachers and students are meagre.

There are parents' meetings twice a year but parents are welcome at any time. There are also home-school notebooks. Parents of the Grade 1 children bring them to school; the other children use the ordinary buses. The school serves just one District so the children do not live far away. Most of their families have lived in the area for generations because, although people are sent off to different places to work, their family base rarely changes.

If parents are unhappy about referral to a special school, no pressure is put on them. There is a long waiting list. If children remain in ordinary schools they may be able to join a special class but these classes are run as separate units and there is no additional support for pupils in mainstream classes. There are pupils, therefore, who stay in their elementary (primary) school until they are 16 or until they drop out.

Zhi Ling Special School for 'Mentally Handicapped' Children, Tien Hao District, Guangzhou

This school is formally recognized by the Education Department of Guangzhou (Canton) but it is a private school, the only one of its kind in the country. Funding comes from Hong Kong Caritas, parents, parents' work units, the China Welfare Fund for Handicapped People, Guangzhou Treasury Department, a local commercial enterprise and the local Welfare Fund. Parents pay fees, which cover daily running expenses, while the Hong Kong money pays for equipment and teacher training. This includes time spent by Guangzhou teachers in Hong Kong special schools. However, the school still runs at a loss, though I do not know how they deal with this.

Most of the children and young people at the school experience 'moderate difficulties in learning', as in the Shanghai school, but there were some pupils whose difficulties were clearly more severe.

Assessments are carried out by educational psychologists from Hong Kong and usually involve IQ testing. Local parents had actively campaigned to have the school opened and there is a waiting list from throughout Guangdong Province and beyond. We learned that the teachers do some outreach work with families whose children are on the waiting list.

Many children with physical disabilities or who experience serious difficulties in learning remain outside the education system at the moment in China, making the Zhi Ling special school particularly attractive. There are very few mobility aids, personal wheelchairs or adapted vehicles. People do not have cars and they cannot afford taxis. Weekly boarding is common in a wide range of pre-school and educational provisions. The only mobility aids I saw were adult tricycles (pedalled and mechanical) and a couple of large buggies, used by children with cerebral palsy at the Zhi Ling school.

Meng Wei Na, the headteacher, gave us a formal introduction to the school and its work and some notes in English prepared for the Beijing conference. She made a point of saying to us that we would see the real thing on this visit, not the public relations exercise we would get in a State school.

Space and buildings are scarce. The school is not purpose-built and is intermingled with the surrounding flats. In China, there are no clear boundaries between plots of land, which I assumed was to do with public ownership and with the absence of any mechanism for debating new building projects. The school has very little equipment. The children sit at desks doing simple activities. As in all the schools I visited, there were noticeably more boys than girls. Here, they sit separately and have their own dormitories and dining rooms. They were all very excited to see us.

Meng Wei Na's notes stress love, happiness and health, as well as practical skills and knowledge. The aims of the school are equality of educational rights and opportunities, the 'full development of human potentiality' and 'the spirit and civilization of Socialism, which is to let "normal" and "mentally handicapped" develop mutual help and love with each other'.

There are about 140 pupils, aged between 4 and 18, with fifty teachers and other workers. Many of the teachers are ex-factory workers, untrained but committed and the school utilizes voluntary staff. I believe that 'voluntary' does not mean unpaid but that workers have chosen to come to the school rather than be assigned work by their local authority.

The curriculum includes: sensory-motor training, self-care

training, social skills, language, mathematics, integrated studies (environmental studies; daily living), practical work, vocational training, music, art and craft, gross motor skills and physical education. The teaching approach is described as 'unidimensional', combining 'knowledge of various subjects together organized systematically according to students' needs and abilities'. Teachers are to encourage their students to learn from direct experience 'through interesting activities' and participate as much as they can. Behaviour modification by means of rewards and punishments is used so that 'education and regulation work hand in hand'.

While she is aware that a 'totally volunteer agency' cannot be incorporated into the state education system at the moment, Meng Wei Na would like to think that the Zhi Ling school will encourage the expansion of provision across the country and that explicit policy making will follow: 'a precise direction of special education with multiple channels, structures and formats . . . set up so that we have various schools for special education which are supported either by government, society or non-governmental organization' (Meng Wei Na, 1988).

Xianshi Mangya Xuexiao — Xian No.1 Deaf School

This school was founded in 1949 after Liberation and is state run. There are about 215 pupils in the Deaf-Mute Department and twenty-five in the Blind Department. Although the government has paid more attention to special education recently and increased the resources available, these have not been directed towards supporting pupils within the mainstream. There are no classes for deaf-mute or blind pupils in ordinary schools.

Pupils are aged between 8 (or 7, as Chinese children are 1 at birth) and 16. Nearly all of them will get a job when they leave. Some students will go on to higher education, a few to a regular university and some to the Chinese equivalent of our Open University, following correspondence or television-based courses.

The school's curriculum includes: Chinese, mathematics, physical education, art, language (English, probably), a 'virtue' course, and vocational training — painting and handicrafts for the deaf students and 'curing the diseases' for the blind students. Students also go out to a relevant workplace for experience before they leave. The school aims to develop the students' independence, to encourage communication between the students themselves and to develop a wider network of parental support.

There is little technology in the schools for deaf children; an exception is the Beijing No. 1 school. At the Xian school only the class for partially-hearing pupils had any technological equipment. The children were wearing headphones and the teacher was using a microphone and a series of prepared tapes. She had recording and amplification systems.

The activities we saw were formal, repetitive, rythmic, based on the textbooks of the National Curriculum, with all pupils doing the same thing at the same time. Boys and girls sit separately in the classrooms, except in the class for partially-hearing children, where they were arranged by height in a semi-circle, from small to tall and back again.

This school has an oral approach but the children were signing in the playground. The staff described their approach as 'total communication' but we did not see much evidence of signing in the classrooms and we heard a lot of children trying their hardest to speak. There are no deaf or blind teachers in the school. However, it seems that there are debates going on about deaf education in China which are just like those which rage in Britain. In a special school in Chongqing there is a deaf teacher and teacher training is offered in the vocational programme (Callaway, 1986). The Xian No. 1 Deaf School is large, though, and we had the feeling that it is a show school. We were told that there is a long waiting list, although there is a second school in Xian city and three more in Shaanxi Province. Teacher education takes place in the school, which trains teachers for the whole of North-West China. There is no formal referral system to the school and the school itself prepares an assessment for the children's parents.

There are sixty-nine members of staff. Amazingly good staff: student ratios were often quoted to us. A London English teacher who spent 1984-5 teaching in Beijing was intrigued by these figures, particularly as the size of mainstream classes remains very large. She discovered that teachers in a middle (secondary) school she visited on two occasions were timetabled for between twelve and sixteen class contact hours out of a forty-eight hour week. They were expected to spend a great deal of time preparing their lessons and the younger teachers had to submit detailed follow-up scripts of each one. She concluded that the rest of the time was spent on administration or other jobs in the school. Teachers undertake a range of duties in China — educational, pastoral (including home visiting during school holidays) and administrative. Their own professional education is school-based and, to a significant extent, self-directed (Plackett, 1987).

Chao Yang Correctional School, Beijing

The first correctional school in China was opened in 1955. The Director of the Chao Yang School was the original school's first Director. Opened in 1987, the Chao Yang School admits pupils aged between 13 and 17. Their behavioural problems include: stealing, fighting, sexual offences and 'mischief'; problems not serious enough to warrant prison. The school sets out to reform rather than punish its pupils and the teachers said that they were successful, with only 7 per cent of the pupils committing further offences.

Teenagers are referred to the school from the ordinary schools, by their parents or by the local authority. The consent of parents and the young person is necessary but the school can force attendance by using the threat of a jail sentence. Pupils stay in the school for a minimum of two years. There are up to thirty-five pupils in a class, many more than in the other kinds of special school, and they divide their time between educational and pre-vocational activities. The educational curriculum is the same as that in the ordinary schools but the students' attainment levels tend to be low for their age. There is more emphasis on moral development and vocational training than on academic progress.

There were 112 students in the school last June, six boys' classes and one girls' class. They have different programmes of work. The students are residential, going home for the holidays but taking part in organized activities in the summer vacation. The school was not full when we visited, which was just after graduation, and there are places for 200 students.

The students' daily routine involves: 6.00 am PE, cleaning the school building, breakfast, four academic lessons, lunch, a rest, three pre-vocational lessons or labouring, recreation or PE, supper, homework and, finally, meetings or talks, counselling and political education. The workshops attached to the school are for electrical engineering, sewing and carpentry. There is a students' club for the informal presentation of their views and they participate in making decisions about school events.

I photographed various notices that I saw around the school which my Mandarin teacher has translated for me. They turn out to be rules and regulations: for the dining-room, the auditorium, the classroom and for secondary school students' daily behaviour. They are mostly about being clean, tidy, quiet, and industrious. The dormitory regulations are more explicitly moral, urging the students to resist the corruption of 'unsuitable social activities and conversations' and 'valueless books'.

For a student to be discharged from the school there has to be a favourable school board assessment and good reports of the student's work and behaviour. The residential committee in their home area will then help them to find a job.

There are fifty-one members of staff at the school, a figure that includes the management committee. The teachers have come from the mainstream; some are untrained but very experienced teachers and some have attended a course at the Beijing Normal University.

We asked if there was any recognition or treatment of emotional problems, as distinct from problems of behaviour. The teachers answered that the students who attend correctional schools are not emotionally disturbed. We were told that the different correctional schools shared the same philosophy but that techniques could vary from school to school There are six correctional schools in Beijing and ninety-three in China as a whole.

Some of the conference delegates who were in the group visiting the Chao Yang School had also visited the Xicheng District 'Workstudy' School. This school was opened in 1978 and there are about 100 students with 130 teachers and workers. The delegates agreed that the formal introductions we were given in the two schools were similar but that the atmosphere was very different. At Chao Yang it was much warmer and more relaxed. They had found the other school military in character and the Principal had appeared authoritarian. Their discussion had not been as open as it was at Chao Yang. The 'Workstudy' School Principal had made it clear that there was one right way to behave and had explicitly referred to the values of the Communist Party. The Party was never mentioned in our conversations at Chao Yang.

We had watched the girls' class rehearse some dancing and singing that they were preparing for their summer school. We were struck by the warmth and informality of the relationships between the teachers and the students. I thought that the dance teacher was a student until she introduced herself. One of the dancers was the President of the students' club. She led the group in a song, which we learned was about peace.

Conclusion

I have described four out of the eight educational and other provisions that I visited and of course none of them is typical. They are to be found in major cities, where only 20 per cent of Chinese people live, and they are all known for their pioneering or exceptional qualities. For many thousands of children with disabilities or who experience difficulties in learning no special educational provision is available at all. They live in remote areas or they have no practical means of getting into school.

It is hard for us in the West to imagine the scale of an education system that could respond appropriately to every child and young person in the world's most populated country. I also discovered that Chinese special educators know far more about European and American systems than most of us know about theirs. Many of them admire our mixed ability teaching, our peripatetic support services, our mainstream resource bases and our differentiated curricula. They acknowledge the straight-jacketing effect of their National Curriculum. Replying, I had to confess that in Britain we are about to scrap all that, develop a National Curriculum . . .

References

BROWN, L.B. (1981) *Psychology in Contemporary China,* Oxford, Pergamon.

CALLAWAY, A. (1986) 'Educating Deaf Children', *China Now,* 116, pp.24-5.

CHENG, KAI MING (1986) 'China's Recent Education Reform: the beginning of an overhaul', *Comparative Education,* 22, 3, pp. 255-69.

LIAOWIANG (1985) 'Liaowiang Interviews Deng Pufang on China Welfare Fund', *Joint Publications Reference Service,* CPS-85-039, 26 April, pp. 36-41.

MENG WEI NA (1988) 'A Brief Introduction to Guangzhou Zhi Ling Special School for the Mentally Handicapped', Typescript prepared for the International Conference on Special Education, Beijing, June.

MIRSKY, J. (1988) 'Reformer Zhao set to tumble', *Observer,* 11 September.

PLACKETT, E. (1987) 'A visit to Number 25 Middle School', *China Now,* 122, pp. 13-7.

SHIH, C. (1979) 'Helping Mentally Handicapped Children to Learn', *International Child Welfare Review,* 42, pp. 31-4.

SPARE RIB, 'Special Education for the Disabled in China', January 1987.

WOMEN OF CHINA, December 1986.

ZHANG, X. and SANG, Y. (1986) *Chinese Lives: An Oral History of Contemporary China,* edited for the English edition by JENNER, W.J.F. and DAVIN, D. London, Macmillan, pp. 293-4.

Notes on Contributors

Theresa B. Abang is a Professor of Special Education at the University of Jos, Nigeria. She is interested in questions of policy.

Len Barton is the Head of Department (Academic and Professional Development) in the Department of Education at Bristol Polytechnic, England. He is Editor of the International Journal Disability, Handicap and Society and the organizer of the Conference at which these papers were initially given.

Jan Branson is a lecturer in the School of Education at La Trobe University, Australia. She is currently involved in research into the question of integration.

Susan Foster is a Research Associate at the National Technical Institute for the Deaf, one of nine colleges of Rochester Institute of Technology, United States. She is the author of *The Politics of Caring*, (Falmer Press). Her areas of interest include educational policy and practice for deaf students and the attainments of deaf adults in the workplace.

Gillian Fulcher currently teaches and researches in sociology at Monash University, Australia. Her book, *Disabling Policies? A Comparative Approach to Education Policy and Disability,* is due to be published by Falmer Press in 1989.

David Galloway is a lecturer in educational research at the University of Lancaster, England. He is the author of *Schools, Pupils and Special Educational Needs* (Croom Helm).

Jan Goodall has experience in general and psychiatric hospital social work. She was a lecturer in Social Work at the University of Dundee for ten years, and became a research fellow there in 1986.

Don Miller is a lecturer in the Department of Anthropology and Sociology, at Monash University, Australia. He is already involved in research into the question of integration.

Patricia Potts is a member of the special education group at the Open University, England and visited China in June, 1988, to participate in an international conference on special education and look at special educational provisions in a number of cities; a trip sponsored by the Open University and the British Council.

Christine E. Sleeter is an Associate Professor at the University of Wisconsin-Parkside, United States. Her areas of interest include multicultural education, sociology of special education, and race, class, and gender issues in education. She coauthored the books *After the School Bell Rings* (Falmer Press), and *Making Choices for Multicultural Education* (Merrill).

Lise Vislie is Professor at the University of Oslo, Institute for Educational Research, Norway. She was a consultant to OECD/CERI in Paris on the project 'The Education of the Handicapped Adolescent: Integration in the School' (1978-82). She co-authored the book *Integration of Handicapped Pupils into Compulsory Education in Norway* (Universitete Forlaget, Oslo).

Index